Jewish Legends of the Patriarchs & Prophets

Midrashic and Apocryphal Tales Beyond Scripture

Rediscover Adam, Noah, Abraham, Moses, and More Through Ancient Hebrew Lore

A Modern Translation

Adapted for the Contemporary Reader

Various Ancient Jewish Writers

Translated by Tim Zengerink

Table of Contents

Preface - Message to the Reader

What If You Could Help Rebuild the Greatest Library in Human History?

Thousands of years ago, the Library of Alexandria stood as the crown jewel of human achievement — a sanctuary where the collected wisdom of every known civilization was gathered, preserved, and shared freely.

And then, it was lost.

Through fire, conquest, and the slow erosion of time, humanity lost not just books — but ideas, dreams, discoveries, and stories that could have changed the world forever.

Today, the Library of Alexandria lives again — and you are invited to be a part of its restoration.

Our mission is simple yet profound:

To rebuild the greatest library the world has ever known, and to translate all timeless works into every language and dialect, so that no seeker of knowledge is ever left behind again.

By joining our movement to rebuild the modern Library of Alexandria, you become part of an unprecedented mission:

- **Unlimited Access to the Greatest Audiobooks & eBooks Ever Written:**

    Instantly explore thousands of legendary works—Plato, Shakespeare, Jane Austen, Leo Tolstoy, and countless more. All instantly available to read or listen, placing a complete literary universe at your fingertips.

- **Beautiful Paperback & Deluxe Editions at Printing Cost**

  Own any title as an elegant paperback, deluxe hardcover, or stunning collectible boxset—offered to you at true printing cost, delivered straight to your door. Build your personal Library of Alexandria, crafted for beauty, built for durability, and worthy of proud display.

- **Fresh Translations for Modern Readers—in Every Language & Dialect**

  Enjoy timeless masterpieces reimagined in clear, contemporary language—no more outdated phrases or obscure references. Alongside the original versions, we're tirelessly translating these classics into every language and dialect imaginable, ensuring accessibility and understanding across cultures and generations.

- **Join a Global Renaissance of Literature & Knowledge**

  You directly support expanding our library, publishing deluxe editions at true cost, translating works into all global languages, and bringing humanity's greatest stories to people everywhere. By joining today, you're not just preserving a legacy of masterpieces; you set in motion a powerful wave of literary accessibility.

Become a Torchbearer of Knowledge.

Join us for free now at **LibraryofAlexandria.com**

Together, we will ensure that the light of human wisdom never fades again.

With gratitude and a shared love of knowledge,
The Modern Library of Alexandria Team

Visit:

www.libraryofalexandria.com

Or scan the code below:

Introduction

The Hebrew Bible, known in Jewish tradition as the Tanakh, serves as the foundational scripture for Judaism and Christianity alike. It tells the story of a people, a covenant, and a divine narrative that stretches from the creation of the universe to the prophetic warnings of exile and hope. But beyond the canonical accounts, the Jewish imagination preserved a rich tradition of storytelling, interpretation, and expansion. This broader scriptural landscape includes works of midrash, apocrypha, mystical speculation, and narrative elaboration. These writings, sometimes poetic and other times didactic, offer not only theological insights but also compelling visions of biblical characters and events through the lens of later generations.

This volume, Jewish Legends of the Patriarchs & Prophets, brings together some of the most significant of these non-canonical writings, including the Book of Jasher, Ladder of Jacob, Joseph and Asenath, Lives of the Prophets, and the Sefer Yetzirah. These works enrich the biblical narrative, embellishing familiar figures like Adam, Noah, Abraham, Jacob, Joseph, and Moses with imaginative detail, cosmic symbolism, and moral lessons.

Rather than contradicting the Bible, these texts often serve to deepen the stories, filling in narrative gaps and offering context that reflects the ethical, mystical, and cultural concerns of the communities that treasured them. Their authors and transmitters were rabbis, sages, mystics, and scribes who viewed storytelling as a sacred task. Through tales of heroism, trial, divine intervention, and cosmic order, they handed down a vision of the biblical world that is as intellectually rigorous as it is spiritually moving.

The Midrashic Spirit and Legendary Expansion

One of the most enduring traits of Jewish literary tradition is its refusal to leave a story untouched or a verse uninterpreted. The term midrash itself means "to seek" or "to investigate," and this spirit of inquiry underpins countless legendary elaborations on Scripture. The Book of Jasher, for example, is a prime example of a midrashic text. Although mentioned briefly in the Bible (Joshua 10:13 and 2 Samuel 1:18), the extant version of Jasher dates to a much later period and seeks to retell the stories of Genesis and Exodus with additional dialogue, backstories, and divine interventions. Here, Abraham is not just a wandering herdsman but a kingmaker and philosopher; Jacob is not only a patriarch but a strategic warrior; and Joseph's descent into Egypt is paralleled with vivid dramatizations that align him with later heroic figures.

In the Lives of the Prophets, we find brief but evocative biographies of each of Israel's prophetic figures, often concluding with miraculous deeds and martyrdoms. These lives are not strict historical chronicles, but they offer ethical and theological insights into the prophetic calling, martyrdom, and divine inspiration. Elijah becomes a recurring celestial visitor; Jeremiah is portrayed as a seer who foresees destruction and exile in increasingly vivid terms. These portraits shaped Jewish and Christian views of prophecy for centuries.

Joseph and Asenath offers a remarkable addition to the Joseph story, centering not on his dreams or Egyptian rise to power, but on the romantic and spiritual transformation of Asenath, his Egyptian wife. This tale, which emphasizes conversion, chastity, divine visions, and angelic visitations, provided a way for ancient audiences to reconcile Joseph's integration into foreign society with the enduring covenant identity of Israel.

Each of these texts not only preserves tradition but innovates within it. They reflect the questions and anxieties of their time—questions about identity, divine justice, suffering, holiness, and cosmic purpose—and they reframe them through the lives of the patriarchs and prophets.

Mysticism, Cosmic Order, and the Power of Letters

In contrast to the narrative richness of the Book of Jasher or the emotional drama of Joseph and Asenath, the Sefer Yetzirah (Book of Creation) transports us into the realm of Jewish mysticism. This text, one of the oldest surviving Kabbalistic works, seeks to explain how God created the universe—not through physical acts alone, but through speech, mathematics, and metaphysical principles.

According to Sefer Yetzirah, the universe was formed through "32 paths of wisdom": ten sefirot (emanations of divine attributes) and twenty-two Hebrew letters. Each letter is not just a symbol but a living force. The combinations and permutations of these letters generate worlds, angels, time, space, and matter. The mystical significance of speech—God's utterances that bring light, order, and life into being—resonates with the Genesis account but adds layers of philosophical and metaphysical interpretation.

This mystical view of creation would have a profound influence on later Jewish thought, particularly in the Kabbalistic movements of medieval Europe. But even in its earliest forms, Sefer Yetzirah offered a spiritual vision of reality that linked the sacred language of Hebrew to the very fabric of existence.

This interplay between language and creation connects with

broader themes in the apocryphal and midrashic writings—namely, that sacred history is not closed. It continues to unfold in the words, prayers, and imaginations of the faithful. As readers, we are not merely observers of ancient history but participants in a living tradition.

Conclusion: Recovering the Imaginative Depth of Scripture

To read Jewish Legends of the Patriarchs & Prophets is to be reminded that the Bible was never a static text, locked in the past. It has always inspired dialogue, elaboration, and reinvention. These midrashic and apocryphal works are not counterfeits of Scripture but compliments—echoes and expansions that show us how deeply the ancient world revered its heroes, and how profoundly it meditated on the meaning of divine revelation.

Through these writings, we see a more fully human Adam and Eve, whose exile leads to penitence and prophecy. We witness a Jacob who not only wrestles with an angel but climbs a ladder into the mysteries of heaven. We walk with Moses not only as lawgiver but as cosmic prophet. And we hear voices of prophets whose brief appearances in the canonical texts are here illuminated with final speeches, miraculous acts, and heaven-sent dreams.

This volume invites readers to open their minds to the layered world of Jewish imagination—where history blends with legend, and faith kindles the embers of eternal storytelling. Whether you approach these texts as sacred literature, historical curiosity, or spiritual meditation, you will find within them a timeless resonance. The legends of the patriarchs and prophets continue to speak because they were never merely about the past. They are about us—our questions, our hopes, and our unfolding journey with the divine.

Welcome to the untold stories of Genesis and beyond. Welcome to the sacred legends of ancient Israel.

Joseph and Asenath

Introduction to Joseph and Asenath

Joseph and Asenath is a fascinating story that expands on the brief mention in the Bible of Joseph's marriage to Asenath, the daughter of an Egyptian priest, as told in the book of Genesis. This text, often linked to the Apocrypha, explores their relationship in detail, focusing on Asenath's journey as she accepts Joseph's faith and how their love story unfolds.

The story combines Jewish and Hellenistic writing styles and explores themes like repentance, divine guidance, and the blending of different cultures and beliefs. Likely written during the Second Temple period, it provides insight into the interactions between Judaism and the Greco-Roman world at that time.

Including this story in religious literature showcases the depth of ancient storytelling and interpretation. It also reinforces the lasting impact of Joseph's story as a model of faith, righteousness, and the power of reconciliation.

Chapter One

Pharaoh gave Joseph the name Zaphnath-Paaneah because of his ability to reveal secrets. He also gave him Asenath, the daughter of Potipherah, the priest of On, to be his wife. After this, Joseph traveled throughout Egypt.

Before the famine began, Asenath gave birth to two sons. Joseph named them Manasseh and Ephraim while living in Egypt.

In the first year of the seven years of abundance, during the second month, Pharaoh sent Joseph on a journey across the land of Egypt. By the fourth month of that year, on the eighteenth day, Joseph arrived in Heliopolis, where he started gathering all the grain from the land. The harvest was so vast that it was as countless as the sand on the seashore.

In Heliopolis, there was a man named Pentephres, who was one of Pharaoh's most important officials. He was a satrap (a high-ranking leader) and the chief priest of Heliopolis. He was extremely wealthy, wise, and generous, serving as one of Pharaoh's closest advisors.

Pentephres had a daughter named Asenath, who was about eighteen years old. She was tall, graceful, and more beautiful than any other young woman in Egypt. She did not look like the daughters of the Egyptians but resembled the Hebrew women. She was as tall as Sarah, as stunning as Rebecca, and as radiant as Rachel.

Asenath's beauty was known throughout the land, even in the farthest regions. Many young men—sons of lords, governors, and kings—wanted to marry her. Because of this, there was fierce competition, and fights broke out over who would win her hand.

When Pharaoh's oldest son heard about her beauty, he asked his father to let him marry Asenath. He said, "Give me Asenath, the daughter of Pentephres, the priest of Heliopolis, to be my wife."

But Pharaoh refused, saying, "Why would you choose a wife of lower status than yourself? Are you not the ruler of all the earth? No! You are already engaged to the daughter of King Joakim. She is a queen and very beautiful—she will be your wife instead."

Chapter Two

Asenath looked down on all men and thought they were beneath her. No man had ever seen her because her father, Pentephres, had built a tall and grand tower inside his home, where she lived. The top floor of the tower had ten rooms.

The first room was large and beautiful, with a floor made of purple stones and walls decorated with precious gems. The ceiling was covered in gold, and the room was filled with countless Egyptian idols made of gold and silver. Asenath worshiped these idols, feared them, and offered sacrifices to them.

The second room was where she kept her finest clothing and treasures. It contained chests filled with gold, silver, and luxurious garments woven with gold, as well as expensive jewels and fine linens. This room also held all her personal ornaments.

The third room was a storage area, filled with the best crops and produce from the land.

The remaining seven rooms belonged to seven young women, each having her own space. These young women were Asenath's attendants, and they were all the same age as her, having been born on the same night. They were as beautiful as the stars in the sky, and no man or boy had ever been involved with them.

Asenath's main room, where she spent most of her time, had three windows: one facing the courtyard to the east, one looking north onto the street, and another facing south. A golden bed stood in the room, positioned toward the east. It was covered with a luxurious purple blanket woven with gold, decorated with blue embroidery and fine linen. Asenath slept alone in this bed, and no one—man or woman—had ever sat on it.

Outside the tower, there was a large courtyard, surrounded by a tall wall made of massive stone blocks. The courtyard had four iron-covered gates, each guarded by eighteen strong young men.

Inside the courtyard, beautiful trees of every kind had been planted, all filled with ripe fruit, since it was harvest season.

On the right side of the courtyard, there was a spring of fresh water that never stopped flowing. Beneath it, a large cistern collected the water, which then flowed through the middle of the courtyard like a river, watering all the trees.

Chapter Three

On the eighteenth day of the fourth month, Joseph arrived in the district of Heliopolis. As he neared the city, he sent twelve men ahead to deliver a message to Pentephres, the priest of Heliopolis.

Joseph's message said, "May I stay at your house today? It is almost noon, and it is time for the midday meal. The sun is very hot, and I would appreciate some rest under your roof."

When Pentephres heard the message, he was overjoyed and said, "Blessed be the Lord, the God of Joseph." Then he called his steward and said, "Hurry! Prepare the house and make everything ready. Prepare a great feast, for Joseph, the mighty man of God, is coming to visit us today."

Meanwhile, Asenath heard that her father and mother had returned from their country estate. She was excited and said, "I will go see my father and mother, for they have come back from their estate."

She quickly dressed in her finest clothes. She put on a blue linen robe woven with gold and tied a golden belt around her waist. She adorned herself with golden bracelets on her wrists and ankles and wore golden trousers along with a gold necklace around her neck. Her jewelry was decorated with precious stones, each engraved with the names of the Egyptian gods. These names were carved into the stones of her bracelets and other ornaments.

She placed a tiara on her head, wrapped a diadem around her temples, and covered her head with a veil.

Chapter Four

Asenath quickly ran down the stairs from her room at the top of the tower and went to greet her father and mother. Pentephres and his wife were overjoyed to see their daughter, dressed beautifully like a bride of God. They gave her many gifts from their country estate, bringing out the best things they had.

Asenath was delighted with the gifts, which included fruit, grapes, dates, doves, pomegranates, and figs. Everything was fresh and delicious.

Pentephres looked at her and said, "My child."

She replied, "Here I am, my lord."

He said, "Sit here between us; I have something important to tell you." So Asenath sat down between her father and mother.

Pentephres took her right hand in his and said, "My child."

Asenath responded, "What is it, Father?"

Pentephres continued, "Listen, Joseph, the mighty man of God, is coming to visit us today. Pharaoh has made him the ruler over all of Egypt. He is in charge of distributing grain and is saving the country from famine.

Joseph is a man who worships God. He is wise, virtuous, and, like you, he has never been with a woman. He has great knowledge, and God's spirit is with him. The Lord's grace is upon him. So, my child, I will give you to him as his wife. You will be his bride, and he will be your husband forever."

When Asenath heard this, her face turned red with anger, and she became furious. She glared at her father and said,

"Why are you saying this, my lord and father? Why would you treat me like a captive and give me to a man from another land? He was once a runaway and was sold as a slave!

Isn't he just a shepherd's son from Canaan, abandoned by his own family? Didn't he get accused of being with his master's wife and then thrown into prison, left in darkness until Pharaoh freed him because he explained a dream? No! I will marry the king's eldest son because he is the true ruler of the world."

Hearing this, Pentephres decided not to say anything more about Joseph, realizing that his daughter was too proud and angry to listen.

Chapter Five

One of Pentephres's young servants suddenly ran in and shouted, "Joseph is at the gates of our courtyard!"

As soon as Asenath heard this, she quickly left her father and mother, ran upstairs to her room, and stood at the large window facing east. From there, she watched as Joseph entered her father's house.

Pentephres, his wife, and all their relatives went out to welcome Joseph. The eastern gates of the courtyard were opened, and Joseph entered, riding in Pharaoh's chariot of honor. The chariot was pulled by four white horses, as pure as snow, with golden reins, and it was covered in shining gold.

Joseph was dressed in a magnificent white tunic, and over it, he wore a purple robe woven with gold. On his head was a golden crown decorated with twelve precious stones, and above them were twelve golden rays shining like the sun. In his right hand, he held a royal scepter.

Joseph also carried an olive branch, full of ripe fruit.

As Joseph entered the courtyard, the gates were shut behind him. No strangers—neither men nor women—were allowed inside, and the gatekeepers locked the doors.

Pentephres, his wife, and all their relatives—except Asenath—stepped forward and bowed down to Joseph, pressing their faces to the ground.

Joseph then stepped down from his chariot and reached out his right hand to greet them.

Chapter Six

Asenath saw Joseph and was completely overwhelmed. Her stomach turned, her knees felt weak, and her whole body trembled. Fear filled her heart, and she cried out,

"Where can I go? Where can I hide from him? How will Joseph, the son of God, even look at me, knowing the terrible things I said about him?

Where can I run and hide when he sees everything, and no secret is hidden from him because of the great light within him? May Joseph's God have mercy on me, for I spoke against him without understanding the truth.

What hope is there for me now? How foolish I was! Didn't I say that Joseph was just a shepherd's son from Canaan? But now I see the truth—he shines like the sun, and today, he has entered our home in all his glory.

I was reckless and arrogant to speak badly about him. I didn't realize that Joseph is truly the son of God.

What man could ever be born with such beauty, and what mother could give birth to someone so radiant? I was blind and foolish to insult him in front of my father.

Now, let my father give me to Joseph as a servant and a slave, and I will serve him for the rest of my life."

Chapter Seven

Joseph entered Pentephres's house and sat down. After washing his feet, a separate table was set before him because he would not eat with the Egyptians, as their customs were different from his own.

Looking toward the window, Joseph asked, "Who is that woman standing in the sunlight? Tell her to leave."

He said this because he was cautious. Many of the wives and daughters of Egypt's nobles and officials had tried to win his attention. Because Joseph was very handsome, they often longed for him, and some even sent messengers with gold, silver, and expensive gifts, hoping he would notice them.

But Joseph always refused, saying, "I will not sin against the God of Israel." He kept his father Jacob's teachings in his heart, remembering the words his father often told him and his brothers:

"My sons, stay away from immoral women, for they lead to destruction."

That was why Joseph said, "Tell that woman to leave."

Pentephres answered, "My lord, the woman you saw is not a stranger. She is our daughter, a virgin who wants nothing to do with men. No man has ever seen her—until today. If you wish, she can come speak with you, for she is like your sister."

When Joseph heard this, he was pleased and said, "If she is your daughter, let her come. From today, I will consider her my sister."

Chapter Eight

Asenath's mother went upstairs to her room and brought her down to meet Joseph. Pentephres said to his daughter, "Greet your brother, for he is also pure, just as you are today. He avoids foreign women, just as you avoid foreign men."

Asenath turned to Joseph and said, "May you be joyful, my lord, for you are blessed by God Most High."

Joseph replied, "May God, who gives life to everything, bless you."

Then Pentephres said to Asenath, "Come closer and kiss your brother."

As Asenath stepped forward to kiss Joseph, he held out his right hand, placed it on her chest, and stopped her. He said,

"It is not right for a man who worships God, who praises the living God with his mouth, eats the blessed bread of life, drinks the holy cup of immortality, and is anointed with sacred oil, to kiss a woman who blesses lifeless idols with her mouth.

A woman like that eats from their table—the bread of sorrow—drinks from their cups, which lead to betrayal, and is anointed with oil that brings destruction.

A man of God may kiss his mother, his sister from his own people, or the wife who shares his life, for these women bless the living God with their mouths. In the same way, a woman who follows God should never kiss a foreign man, for this is unacceptable in God's eyes."

When Asenath heard Joseph's words, she was heartbroken. She began to cry loudly, and tears filled her eyes as she looked at him.

Joseph saw her sadness and felt compassion for her. He was kind, merciful, and full of reverence for God.

He lifted his right hand over her head and prayed,

"O Lord, the God of my father Israel, the Most High, the Mighty One, who gives life to all things, who calls them out of darkness into light, out of confusion into truth, and out of death into life, bless and renew this young woman with Your Spirit.

Transform her with Your unseen hand and give her new life. May she eat the bread of life and drink from Your cup of blessing. You chose her even before she was born. May she enter the rest You have prepared for those You have chosen."

Chapter Nine

Asenath felt overwhelming joy after Joseph blessed her. She quickly went up to her room at the top of the tower and collapsed onto her couch, completely exhausted. While she was happy, she also felt uneasy and deeply afraid. Her whole body was covered in sweat from the moment Joseph spoke to her in the name of God Most High.

She began to cry bitterly and regretted worshiping her old gods. She waited for evening to come, lost in her thoughts.

Meanwhile, Joseph finished eating and drinking, then said to his servants, "Hitch the horses to the chariot. I must leave now and travel through the city and the surrounding area."

Pentephres turned to Joseph and said, "Please, my lord, stay the night with us and leave in the morning."

But Joseph replied, "No, I must go now, for today is the day when God first began His works. In eight days, I will return and stay the night with you."

Chapter Ten

Then Pentephres and his family returned to their estate, leaving Asenath alone with her attendants. But Asenath felt restless and cried until sunset. She refused to eat or drink, and while everyone else slept, she stayed awake.

She quietly opened the door and went down to the gate, where she found the gatekeeper asleep with her children. Moving quickly, she took down the leather curtain from the door, filled it with ashes, carried it back to her room at the top of the tower, and spread the ashes across the floor. She then locked the door with an iron bar and began weeping loudly.

One of the young women who was closest to Asenath heard her sobbing. She woke the others, and together they went to Asenath's door, but they found it locked. Hearing her cries, they called out, "Why are you so sad, my lady? What's wrong? Open the door so we can help you."

Asenath answered from inside, "I have a terrible headache and am lying down. I don't have the strength to open the door because I'm so exhausted. Please go back to your rooms."

Later, Asenath got up, quietly unlocked her door, and went into her second room, where she kept her fine clothes and treasures. She opened her wardrobe and took out a black mourning tunic, the one she had worn when her oldest brother died. She removed her royal robe and put on the black tunic. She untied her golden belt and replaced it with a simple rope around her waist. She also took off her tiara, diadem, and bracelets.

Then, she picked up her finest royal robe and threw it out the window for the poor. Next, she gathered all her gold and silver idols, broke them into small pieces, and tossed them outside for the needy.

Asenath also took her royal feast—the meats, fish, and offerings meant for her gods—along with the wine vessels used in their ceremonies, and threw them out the window as food for the dogs. Afterward, she spread the ashes all over her floor.

She put on sackcloth, tied it around her waist, took the band from her hair, and sprinkled ashes over herself. Then she lay down in the ashes, beating her chest and crying bitterly through the night.

By morning, Asenath saw that the ashes beneath her were soaked with tears, turning them into mud. She fell face down into them again and stayed there until sunset.

Asenath continued this for seven days, refusing to eat or drink.

Chapter Eleven

On the eighth day, Asenath lifted her head from the floor where she had been lying. Her body had become weak from the many days of suffering.

Chapter Twelve

Aseneth reached out her hands toward the east and looked up to the sky, saying:

"O Lord, God of all time, You gave life to everything. You brought things that were hidden into the light and created all that exists. You raised the heavens and placed the earth upon the waters. You set the great stones in the sea so they would not sink but remain as You commanded.

O Lord, my God, I call out to You. Please hear me, and I will admit all my sins. I will confess everything I have done wrong.

I have sinned, Lord—I have disobeyed Your law and done evil. I have spoken wicked things in Your presence. My mouth has been made unclean by eating food offered to idols and by sitting at the table of the Egyptian gods.

I have worshiped lifeless idols that cannot hear or speak. I do not deserve to speak to You, for I am full of shame. I, Aseneth, daughter of Pentephres the priest, was proud and arrogant, and I have done wrong.

Now, Lord, I lift my prayer to You and cry out for help. Save me from those who want to harm me! I run to You like a child seeking protection from their parents.

Reach out to me, Lord, like a father who loves and protects his children. Rescue me from the hands of my enemy.

A fierce and ancient lion is chasing me—his children are the Egyptian gods I rejected and destroyed. Their father, the Devil, wants to destroy me.

But You, Lord, are my only hope. Save me from his grip! Do not let him take me like a wolf catching its prey. Do not let him throw me into fire or deep waters. Do not let the great sea creature swallow me whole.

Lord, I am alone. My father and mother have turned away from me because I destroyed their gods. But I trust in You alone. You are the Father of orphans, the protector of those who are hunted, and the helper of those who suffer.

All my father's gods are weak and temporary, but those who belong to You, Lord, will last forever."

Chapter Thirteen

Look at me, Lord—I am alone, with no family to turn to, so I have come to You for shelter.

I have taken off my royal robe, woven with gold, and put on a simple black garment instead. I removed my golden belt and tied a rough rope and sackcloth around my waist. I took the crown from my head and covered myself in ashes.

The floor of my room, once decorated with colorful stones and purple fabrics and filled with the scent of myrrh, is now soaked with my tears and covered in ashes. The mixture of my tears and ashes has turned into mud, making my room look like a street walked by many.

I gave away my royal feast and the finest meats to the dogs. For seven days and nights, I have eaten nothing and drunk no water. My mouth is as dry as a drum, my tongue stiff like a horn, my lips cracked like broken pottery. My face is thin, and my eyes are weak from crying nonstop.

But, Lord, please forgive me. I sinned without knowing the truth. I spoke wrongly about my lord Joseph because I did not realize who he really was.

I was told he was just the son of a shepherd from Canaan, and I believed it. I was blind to the truth and looked down on him, not knowing that he is Your chosen one.

Who has ever been as handsome as Joseph? Who else is as wise and strong? But now, Lord, I place him in Your hands, for I love him more than my own life.

Please keep him in Your wisdom and grace. And if it is Your will, let me serve him—I will wash his feet, care for him, and be his servant for the rest of my days.

Chapter Fourteen

As Aseneth finished her prayer and confessed her sins to the Lord, the morning star rose in the eastern sky.

When she saw it, joy filled her heart, and she said, "The Lord has heard me! This star is His messenger, bringing news of a new and glorious day."

Suddenly, the sky around the morning star opened up, and a brilliant light appeared, unlike anything she had ever seen.

Overcome with awe, Aseneth fell face-down into the ashes. Then, a man came down from heaven and stood beside her.

He called out, "Aseneth."

She was startled and said, "Who is calling me? My door is shut, and my tower is high—how could anyone have entered my room?"

The man spoke again, "Aseneth, Aseneth."

She replied, "Here I am, my lord. Please, tell me who you are."

He answered, "I am the leader of the Lord's house, the commander of all His armies. Stand up, and I will speak to you."

Aseneth lifted her head and saw a man who looked exactly like Joseph. He wore a royal robe, a crown, and carried a staff.

But his face shone like lightning, his eyes blazed like the sun, his hair looked like burning fire, and his hands and feet glowed like heated iron.

Aseneth trembled with fear and fell to the ground at his feet.

The man said, "Do not be afraid, Aseneth. Stand up and listen to my words."

She rose to her feet, and he continued, "Take off the black robe you are wearing and remove the sackcloth from your waist. Brush the ashes from your head and wash your face with water.

Put on a new robe, one that has never been worn before, and fasten the bright double belt of your purity around your waist."

Then he added, "When you have done this, return to me, and I will share the message I was sent to give you."

Aseneth went into the room where she kept her fine clothes and treasures. She opened her wardrobe, took out a beautiful, clean robe, and replaced her black tunic with it.

She untied the rough rope and sackcloth from her waist and fastened the shining double belt of her purity—one piece around her waist and the other across her chest.

Then, she shook the ashes from her head, washed her face with pure water, and covered her head with a fine, elegant veil.

24

Chapter Fifteen

Aseneth returned to the man, and when he saw her, he said, "Take off your veil, for today you are pure, and your head is like that of a young person."

She removed her veil, and the man continued, "Be strong, Aseneth, for the Lord has heard your prayers and confession.

Do not be afraid, for your name is now written in the book of life, and it will never be removed. From this day on, you are made new, given a fresh start, and blessed with a new life. You will eat the bread of life, drink from the cup of eternity, and be anointed with oil that never fades.

Take heart, Aseneth, for the Lord has chosen you to be Joseph's wife, and he will be your husband.

Your name will no longer be Aseneth but 'City of Refuge,' because many nations will find safety in you. Under your protection, many people will take shelter, and within your walls, those who turn to God will find peace.

For Penitence, the daughter of the Most High, is always pleading for you and for everyone who repents. The Most High is her Father, and she is the mother of those who remain pure. She prays every moment for those who turn back to God and has prepared a heavenly wedding chamber for those who love her. She watches over them forever.

Penitence is pure, beautiful, and gentle. The Most High treasures her, and all His angels honor her.

Now, I am going to Joseph to speak to him about you. He will come to see you today, and he will rejoice because you will be his bride.

Listen carefully, Aseneth: put on your wedding dress—the special robe that was kept in your room. Wear your finest jewelry and prepare yourself as a bride, for Joseph is coming to see you today, and when he does, he will be filled with joy."

When the man finished speaking, Aseneth's heart overflowed with happiness.

She fell at his feet and said, "Blessed is the Lord who sent you to rescue me from darkness and bring me into the light. May His name be praised forever.

Please, my lord, if I have found favor with you, stay a little while. Sit on my bed, and I will prepare a meal for you. I will bring you the finest wine before you continue on your journey."

Chapter Sixteen

The man said to her, "Please bring me a honeycomb as well."

Aseneth replied, "Let me send someone to my family's estate in the countryside to bring one for you, my lord."

The man said, "Go into your inner room, and you will find a honeycomb there."

Aseneth went into her inner room and, just as he said, found a honeycomb sitting on the table. It was pure white, overflowing with honey, and its scent was sweet and fresh, like the breath of life itself.

She picked it up and brought it to the man. He looked at her and said, "Why did you say there was no honeycomb in your house? Yet now you have brought me this."

Aseneth answered, "My lord, I truly had no honeycomb here

before. It appeared just as you said. Could it have come from you? Its fragrance is as rich as myrrh."

The man placed his hand on her head and said, "You are blessed, Aseneth, because God's mysteries have been revealed to you. Blessed also are those who turn to the Lord in repentance, for they will eat from this honeycomb.

The bees of Paradise have made this honey, and the angels of God eat from it. Anyone who eats it will never die."

Then the man stretched out his right hand, broke off a piece of the honeycomb, and ate it. He took another piece and placed it in Aseneth's mouth.

Next, he reached out his hand and touched the edge of the honeycomb that faced east. The path of his finger turned red, like blood.

Then he stretched his hand again and touched the edge facing north. Once more, the trail of his finger turned to blood.

Aseneth stood beside him, watching everything.

Suddenly, bees began to emerge from the honeycomb's cells. They were as white as snow, and their wings shimmered with shades of purple, blue, and gold. Tiny golden crowns rested on their heads, and they had sharp stingers.

The bees flew in circles around Aseneth, from her feet to her head. Larger bees, nearly the size of queen bees, gently rested on her lips.

The man spoke to them, "Go now to your places."

Immediately, the bees left Aseneth, fell to the ground, and lay still.

Then the man said, "Get up now and return to your places."

At his words, the bees rose up and flew away, each one heading toward the courtyard around Aseneth's tower.

Chapter Seventeen

The man looked at Aseneth and said, "Did you see that?"

She replied, "Yes, my lord, I saw everything."

He nodded and said, "Just as you have seen, so it will be with the words I have spoken to you."

Then he reached out and touched the honeycomb. Suddenly, fire rose up from the table and burned it completely. As it burned, a fresh and sweet fragrance filled the entire room.

Aseneth turned to the man and said, "My lord, I have seven young women who were raised with me and serve me. They were born on the same night as I was, and I love them like sisters. Please, let me call them so that you may bless them as you have blessed me."

The man said, "Call them."

Aseneth quickly summoned the seven virgins, and when they arrived, the man blessed them, saying, "May God, the Most High, bless you forever."

Then he turned to Aseneth and said, "Take this table away."

As she turned to move it, the man suddenly disappeared from her sight. She looked up and saw something like a fiery chariot rising into the sky, heading east.

Overcome with awe, Aseneth whispered, "Have mercy on me, Lord, for I spoke wrongly before You without understanding."

Chapter Eighteen

As this was happening, a young man, one of Joseph's servants, arrived and said, "Look! Joseph, the great man of God, is coming to see you today."

Aseneth quickly called her steward and said, "Prepare a special meal for me, because Joseph, the mighty man of God, will be visiting us."

Then she went into her room and opened her wardrobe. She took out her finest robe, which shimmered like lightning, and put it on.

Around her waist, she tied a dazzling royal belt decorated with precious stones.

She put golden bracelets on her wrists, slipped golden sandals onto her feet, and placed an expensive necklace around her neck.

On her head, she set a golden crown, its front decorated with the most precious gems.

Finally, she covered her head with a veil.

Turning to her maidservant, she said, "Bring me fresh water from the spring."

Aseneth bent over the basin made of polished shell, and as she looked into the water, her face glowed like the sun, and her eyes sparkled like the morning star at dawn.

Chapter Nineteen

A young servant came to Aseneth and said, "Joseph has arrived and is waiting at the gates of the courtyard."

Aseneth quickly went down with her seven attendants to meet

him.

When Joseph saw her, he said, "Come to me, pure one, for I have received a message from heaven telling me everything about you."

Joseph reached out his hands and embraced Aseneth, and she held him tightly in return. They greeted each other with warmth and joy, their hearts filled with new life.

Chapter Twenty

Aseneth said to Joseph, "Come inside, my lord, and be welcome in my home." She gently took his right hand and led him inside.

Joseph sat down in the seat of her father, Pentephres, while Aseneth brought water to wash his feet.

Joseph said, "Let one of your attendants wash my feet."

But Aseneth shook her head and replied, "No, my lord. Your feet are as my own, and your hands are mine. No one else will do this for you."

She insisted and washed his feet herself.

Joseph then took her right hand and kissed it, and Aseneth, in return, kissed his head.

Later that day, Aseneth's parents returned from their country estate. When they saw her sitting beside Joseph, dressed in a wedding robe, they were overjoyed. They praised God and joined them for a meal, eating and drinking together.

Pentephres turned to Joseph and said, "Tomorrow, I will invite the nobles and rulers of Egypt to celebrate your wedding, and you shall take Aseneth as your wife."

Joseph replied, "First, I must speak with Pharaoh about Aseneth, for he is like a father to me. He will officially give his blessing for me to marry her."

Joseph stayed that night in Pentephres's house, but he did not sleep with Aseneth. He said, "It would not be right for a man who serves God to be with his wife before they are married."

Chapter Twenty One

Joseph woke up early in the morning and sent a message to Pharaoh, telling him about Aseneth.

Pharaoh immediately called for Pentephres and Aseneth to come to his palace.

When he saw Aseneth, he was amazed by her beauty and said, "The Lord, the God of Joseph, will bless you. He has chosen you to be Joseph's wife. Joseph is God's firstborn son, and you will be called the daughter of the Most High. Joseph will be your husband forever."

Pharaoh then took golden crowns and placed them on their heads, saying, "May God Most High bless you and make your family strong and prosperous for all time."

He turned them toward each other, and they kissed.

Pharaoh then held a grand wedding celebration, hosting a huge feast that lasted for seven days. He invited all the important officials and rulers of Egypt to join in the festivities.

He also issued a royal decree, saying, "Anyone who works during the seven days of Joseph and Aseneth's wedding will be put to death."

After the wedding and celebrations ended, Joseph and Aseneth were together, and she became pregnant. She later gave birth to two sons, Manasseh and his younger brother, Ephraim, in Joseph's household.

Chapter Twenty Two

After the years of plenty came to an end, the seven years of famine began to spread across the land. The hunger reached many nations, and people struggled to find food.

When Jacob heard that his son Joseph was alive and ruling in Egypt, he gathered his family and all their belongings and traveled there. They arrived in Egypt during the second month, on the twenty-first day, and settled in the fertile land of Goshen, which had been set aside for them.

One day, Aseneth said to Joseph, "I want to meet your father, because your father Israel is now my father too."

Joseph smiled and said, "Then let's go together to see him."

They set out for Goshen, and as they neared their destination, Joseph's brothers came out to greet them. They bowed deeply to Joseph and Aseneth as a sign of respect.

When they arrived at Jacob's tent, he welcomed them with open arms, blessing them and kissing them with great affection.

Aseneth embraced Jacob, wrapping her arms around his neck, and kissed him as if he were her own father. Touched by her love and respect, Jacob blessed her warmly and welcomed her into his family with joy.

Later, they all sat down together for a meal, eating and drinking in celebration of their reunion. The gathering was filled with gratitude as they gave thanks to God for bringing them back together after so many years apart.

When it was time for Joseph and Aseneth to return home, Simeon and Levi traveled with them to keep them safe. Levi walked on Aseneth's right side, and Simeon on her left, making sure she was well protected.

Aseneth held Levi's hand as they walked, feeling a special connection with him. She admired him deeply because he was not only a devoted servant of God but also a prophet with great wisdom. Levi had a rare gift—he could see letters written in the heavens, revealing divine messages. He often shared these insights privately with Aseneth, offering her guidance and spiritual understanding.

Levi also had a vision of Aseneth's future, seeing that she would one day rest in the highest heaven, a place of eternal peace and glory. His gift allowed him to understand her destiny and the great blessings that awaited her as someone chosen by God. Their bond was built on faith and a shared devotion to the Lord, making their connection not only one of family but also of deep spiritual friendship.

Chapter Twenty Three

As Joseph and Aseneth were passing by, Pharaoh's eldest son spotted them from the top of a wall. The moment he saw Aseneth, he was struck by her beauty and became consumed with desire for her. Unable to control his emotions, he sent messengers to summon Simeon and Levi. When they arrived, they stood before him, waiting to hear what he had to say.

Pharaoh's son said, "I have heard of your incredible strength and skill in battle. People say no one on earth can match you. I know that with your own hands, you destroyed the city of Shechem and, using just two swords, defeated thirty thousand warriors.

I need your help. Join me without hesitation, and I will reward you with gold, silver, servants, houses, and vast lands. Stand by my side and be loyal to me, for I have been wronged by your brother Joseph. He took Aseneth as his wife, though she was meant to be mine.

Now, come with me, and together we will fight against Joseph. I will strike him down with my sword and take Aseneth as my wife. In return, I will make you my brothers and closest allies forever. But if you refuse, I will kill you both with my sword." As he spoke, he pulled out his sword and waved it in front of them.

Simeon, known for his bravery and quick temper, instantly drew his own sword from its sheath and rushed forward, ready to strike Pharaoh's son.

But Levi, who was a prophet and could see what was about to happen, acted fast. He stepped firmly on Simeon's right foot, stopping him from attacking.

Levi turned to him and said, "Why are you letting your anger take over? We are the sons of a man who follows God, and it is not right for someone who serves Him to repay evil with evil."

Then, Levi looked at Pharaoh's son and spoke calmly and with respect. "My lord, why do you speak to us like this? We are men who worship the Lord, and our father is a servant of God Most High. Our brother Joseph is loved by God. How could we ever commit such a terrible act against him?

Listen carefully—never say such things about our brother again. But if you are determined to go through with this, then know that we are ready."

With that, Simeon and Levi both drew their swords, holding them up for Pharaoh's son to see. Levi continued, "Do you see these swords? These are the very weapons the Lord used to bring justice when the men of Shechem dishonored our sister Dinah, the daughter of Israel."

When Pharaoh's son saw their swords, he was overcome with fear. His whole body shook, and he collapsed to the ground at their feet, terrified.

Levi reached out his hand, helped him up, and said, "Do not be afraid. Just make sure you never speak against our brother again."

Simeon and Levi then left him behind, still trembling with fear.

Chapter Twenty Four

Pharaoh's son was overwhelmed with desire for Aseneth, and his frustration became unbearable. His servants noticed his distress and whispered to him, "The sons of Bilhah and Zilpah, the maidservants of Jacob's wives, Leah and Rachel, dislike Joseph and Aseneth. They are jealous of them and would be more than willing to help you with whatever you plan."

Hearing this, Pharaoh's son immediately sent messengers to summon them in secret. That night, they arrived, and he greeted them, saying, "I have heard that you are strong and skilled warriors."

Gad and Dan, the eldest among them, answered, "Tell us what you need, my lord, and we will do it."

Pleased, Pharaoh's son dismissed his other servants, saying, "Leave us. I have something private to discuss with these men." Once they were alone, he began to deceive them with lies.

"I am offering you a choice—riches and power or death. Choose wisely and live. I know you are brave men who would rather die fighting than live in shame. Now is your chance to take revenge on your enemies.

I overheard Joseph speaking to my father, Pharaoh. He said, 'Dan and Gad are only the sons of maidservants and not my real brothers. I am waiting for my father to pass away so I can deal with them and their descendants. They will not share in our inheritance because they are of lower status. They were the ones who sold me to the Ishmaelites, and I will make sure they pay for it.'

Pharaoh praised Joseph, saying, 'You are right, my son. Take some of my soldiers and punish them as they once did to you. You have my full support.'"

When Gad and Dan heard this, they became furious and said, "We put our trust in you, my lord. Tell us what to do, and we will carry it out."

Pharaoh's son replied, "Tonight, I will kill my father, for he treats Joseph as if he were his own son. You must kill Joseph, and I will take Aseneth as my wife."

Gad and Dan agreed, saying, "We will do whatever you ask. We heard Joseph telling Aseneth, 'Tomorrow, go to our estate for the grape harvest.' He has arranged for six hundred armed soldiers and fifty outrunners to escort her."

When Pharaoh's son heard this, he formed a plan. He placed each of the four men in charge of five hundred soldiers, making them officers and commanders.

Gad and Dan then said, "We will go at night and hide by the brook in the woods. You, my lord, should take fifty horsemen with bows and ride ahead. When Aseneth arrives, she will fall into our trap, and we will ambush her guards.

She will try to escape in her chariot, and that is when you will capture her. Once she is in your hands, we will kill Joseph while he is grieving over her. Then we will kill his children right in front of him."

Pharaoh's son was thrilled with this plan and immediately sent two thousand soldiers to join them. The men reached the brook and hid in the forest along the banks. Five hundred soldiers took position at the front, with a road running between them, setting the perfect trap.

Chapter Twenty Five

Pharaoh's son went to his father's chamber, planning to kill him, but the guards at the entrance refused to let him in.

"I want to see my father before I leave to check on my new vineyards," he told them.

The guards responded, "Your father is not well. He has been in pain all night and is finally resting. He gave us strict orders: 'Do not let anyone enter, not even my eldest son.'"

Frustrated and angry, Pharaoh's son stormed off. Gathering fifty mounted archers, he led them ahead, just as Dan and Gad had suggested.

Meanwhile, Naphtali and Asher confronted their brothers Dan and Gad. "Why are you plotting against our father Israel and our brother Joseph?" they asked. "Don't you see that God protects Joseph like the most precious thing in His sight?

You already sold him as a slave once before, and look at him now—he rules over the land, saves nations, and provides us with food during this famine.

If you try to harm him again, he will surely call upon the God of Israel. The Lord will send fire from heaven to destroy you, and His angels will rise up to fight against you."

Dan and Gad, furious at their brothers' words, snapped back, "Do you expect us to sit here and die like cowards? Never!"

Ignoring Naphtali and Asher's warnings, they pressed forward with their plan, moving ahead to attack Joseph and Aseneth.

Chapter Twenty Six

Aseneth woke up early in the morning and said to Joseph, "I'm going to our estate in the countryside, but I feel afraid because you won't be there with me."

Joseph reassured her, "Be strong and don't be afraid. Go with confidence, for the Lord is with you. He will watch over you and keep you safe, just as He protects what is most precious to Him.

I must stay here to distribute grain and make sure everyone in the city gets food so that no one dies from the famine in Egypt."

With that, Aseneth set off on her journey, while Joseph went to oversee the grain supply.

As Aseneth and her six hundred soldiers reached the brook, Pharaoh's son and his men suddenly launched their ambush. They jumped out from their hiding places and attacked Aseneth's guards. A violent battle broke out, and many of her soldiers were killed. The attackers struck down all her outrunners with their swords.

Seeing the bloodshed, Aseneth panicked and fled in her chariot, racing as fast as she could to escape the chaos.

Meanwhile, Levi, the son of Leah, sensed the danger—being a prophet, he had foreseen the attack. He quickly warned his brothers, and they immediately prepared for battle. Each one grabbed a sword, strapped on a shield, and took up a spear before rushing off at full speed to rescue her.

As Aseneth fled, Pharaoh's son and fifty of his men suddenly appeared in front of her. The moment she saw them, her heart pounded with fear, and she began to tremble, unsure of what would happen next.

Chapter Twenty Seven

Benjamin sat beside Aseneth in the chariot.

He was a strong and handsome young man, about eighteen years old, with the strength of a young lion. His beauty was beyond words, but most importantly, he was a man who feared God.

As the danger grew near, Benjamin sprang from the chariot. He spotted a round stone by the brook, picked it up, and threw it with all his might at Pharaoh's son. The stone struck him hard on the left temple, leaving him badly injured. He fell from his horse, barely clinging to life.

Benjamin then climbed onto a nearby rock and called out to Aseneth's chariot driver, "Bring me fifty stones from the brook." The driver quickly gathered the stones and handed them over.

One by one, Benjamin hurled the stones at Pharaoh's son's fifty men. Every throw hit its mark, striking each soldier in the temple and killing them instantly.

At the same time, the sons of Leah—Reuben, Simeon, Levi, Judah, Issachar, and Zebulun—rushed into the ambush. They attacked with such speed and power that they defeated all two thousand enemy soldiers, wiping them out completely.

Meanwhile, the sons of Bilhah and Zilpah, who had helped with the plot, saw what was happening and ran in fear. As they fled, they shouted to each other, "We're doomed because of our brothers!

Pharaoh's son has been killed by Benjamin, and all his soldiers have died at his hands. We must act fast—let's kill Aseneth and Benjamin before escaping into the woods."

With their swords still dripping with blood, they charged toward Aseneth. When she saw them coming, she cried out in desperation, "O Lord, my God, You saved me from death and promised that my soul would live forever. Please rescue me from these men!"

The Lord heard Aseneth's prayer. In an instant, the swords of her attackers fell from their hands, crumbling into dust as they hit the ground.

Chapter Twenty Eight

The sons of Bilhah and Zilpah saw what had happened and were filled with fear. They turned to each other and said, "The Lord Himself is fighting for Aseneth against us."

Terrified, they fell to the ground before Aseneth and pleaded, "Have mercy on us, for you are our mistress and queen. We have sinned against you and against our brother Joseph. Now God has judged us for our wrongdoing.

Please, spare us and save us from our brothers, for they will surely take revenge on us. Their swords will be turned against us, and we will not escape their anger."

Aseneth, moved by their desperation, spoke gently to them. "Do not be afraid. Your brothers serve God, and they do not repay evil with evil.

But for now, go into the woods to keep yourselves safe. What you have done is no small offense, and I must speak to them on your behalf to calm their anger.

Be strong and do not fear, for the Lord Himself will bring justice between us."

Hearing her words, Dan and Gad quickly fled into the woods.

Just then, the sons of Leah came running like swift deer, chasing after them. Aseneth stepped down from her chariot and went to meet them, tears in her eyes.

Her brothers stopped, bowed before her, and wept. Then they asked where the sons of Bilhah and Zilpah had gone, determined to hunt them down and kill them.

Wiping her tears, Aseneth said, "Spare your brothers and do not harm them. The Lord has already defended me. He turned their swords into dust, and they melted away like wax in fire.

That alone should be enough for us. The Lord has fought for us, so there is no need for revenge. Please, let them live."

Simeon, still furious, replied, "Why do you ask us to spare those who have become our enemies?

No! We must kill them with our swords. This is the second time they have plotted evil—first against our father Israel and our brother Joseph, and now against you."

But Aseneth stood firm. "No, my brother," she said. "Do not repay evil with evil. Leave justice in the hands of the Lord. He will punish them in His own time."

Hearing her words, Simeon lowered his head and bowed to her in respect. Then Levi stepped forward, took Aseneth's right hand, kissed it, and blessed her.

Because of Aseneth's wisdom and kindness, she was able to save the sons of Bilhah and Zilpah from their brothers' anger and prevent their deaths.

Chapter Twenty Nine

Pharaoh's son struggled to sit up from the ground. Blood poured from the wound on his temple, running into his mouth as he coughed and gasped for air, spitting out blood.

Benjamin stepped toward him, gripping Pharaoh's sword and pulling it from its sheath, since he had no weapon of his own. With the sword raised, he prepared to strike him down.

Just as Benjamin was about to deliver the final blow, Levi rushed forward and grabbed his hand. "No, my brother," Levi said firmly. "You must not do this. We are men who serve God, and it is not right to repay evil with evil. It is wrong to strike a man who is already defeated or to chase an enemy to his death.

Instead, let's tend to his wound. If he survives, he may become our ally, and his father, Pharaoh, will continue to treat us as his own family."

Levi then helped Pharaoh's son to his feet, gently washed the blood from his face, and wrapped his wound with a bandage. After making sure he was stable, Levi placed him on his horse and brought him back to Pharaoh.

When they arrived, Levi explained everything that had happened. Pharaoh listened carefully, and when he heard the full story, he was deeply moved. Overcome with gratitude and humility, he stood up from his throne and bowed low to Levi.

Despite their efforts to save him, Pharaoh's son died three days later from the injury caused by the stone Benjamin had thrown. Pharaoh was heartbroken over the loss of his eldest son, filled with sorrow and grief.

His sadness took a toll on his health, and he became weaker. Eventually, Pharaoh passed away at the age of 109. Before his death, he placed the crown of Egypt in Joseph's hands.

Joseph ruled Egypt for 48 years, leading the nation with wisdom and fairness. When his time as king came to an end, he passed the crown to Pharaoh's grandson and guided the young ruler, acting as a father to him as he took on the responsibilities of leading Egypt.

Ladder of Jacob

Jacob went to stay with his uncle Laban. As the sun set, he found a spot to sleep, using a stone as a pillow. That night, he had a dream.

In the dream, he saw a ladder standing on the ground that reached all the way to the sky. At the top of the ladder was a glowing face that looked like it was made of fire and shaped like a person. The ladder had twelve steps, and on each step were two human faces—one on the left and one on the right—making twenty-four faces in total. But one face in the middle was bigger and brighter than the rest. It stretched from the shoulders to the arms and looked more powerful and frightening than any of the others.

As Jacob watched, he saw angels going up and down the ladder. Then he looked up and saw the Lord standing above it. The Lord called out, "Jacob, Jacob!" Jacob replied, "I'm here, Lord." Then the Lord said, "The land you are lying on will belong to you and your children after you. I will make your family as countless as the stars in the sky and the sand by the sea. Because of your family, all the people on earth will be blessed—even in the far future. The blessing I give you will continue for many generations. People from the east and west will be part of your family."

Hearing this made Jacob shake with fear. He woke up, still feeling the presence of God's voice. He said, "This place is holy! It must be God's house and the gate of heaven." Then he took the stone he had used as a pillow, stood it upright as a marker, poured oil over it, and named the place "God's House."

Then he prayed, "Lord God, Creator of Adam, God of Abraham and Isaac, my father, and of all who live faithfully—you sit above the cherubim and rule from a throne that glows with fire and is covered in eyes. You carry the cherubim with four faces, you support the seraphim with many eyes, and you hold the world in your arms while no one holds you. You created the heavens to honor your name and spread the skies above the clouds. You guide the sun and hide it at night so people don't think it's a god. You made a path for the moon and stars. The moon grows and shrinks, and the stars move just as you told them to—so they won't be mistaken for gods either.

The six-winged seraphim stand in front of you. They cover their faces and feet with their wings and fly with the others, singing, 'Holy, Holy, Holy!' You are the Most High with many names. You are fire and lightning, full of glory. You are Jao, Jaoel, Sabakdos, Chabod, Sabaoth, Omlelech, Elaber, and more. You are the eternal King—strong, mighty, patient, and full of greatness. You fill the heavens, the earth, the sea, and even the deepest places with your glory. Please hear my prayer. Listen to my praise. Show me what my dream means. You are strong, holy, and full of glory. You are my God and the God of my fathers."

While Jacob was still praying, a voice appeared in front of him. It said, "Sarekl, leader of those who serve with joy and keeper of visions—go help Jacob understand the dream he saw. Show him everything he saw, but first, bless him."

Then the archangel Sarekl came to Jacob. His face looked powerful, but Jacob wasn't scared. The face he had seen in the dream was even more intense, so he wasn't afraid of the angel. The angel asked, "What is your name?" Jacob answered, "Jacob." Then the angel said, "From now on, you will no longer be called Jacob. Your name will be like mine—Israel."

Later, as Jacob traveled from Fandana in Syria to meet his brother

Esau, Esau came to him, blessed him, and also called him Israel. Esau didn't tell Jacob his own name at first. Only when Jacob begged him did Esau finally share it and explained that it was connected to something Jacob had done. (This part seems to mix up Jacob's dream with the story of when he wrestled the angel, and the details are a little unclear.)

The angel explained, "The ladder you saw with twelve steps and faces on each side stands for the world you're living in now. Each step is a period of time, and the twenty-four faces are the kings who rule over non-believing nations. During their rule, your descendants will suffer because of their sins. The place you saw will be destroyed four times. Still, the temple will be rebuilt to honor the God of your ancestors. But because of their sin, it will be ruined again, and will stay that way until the fourth generation has passed. That's why you saw four visions."

Then Jacob saw someone trip while climbing the ladder. He saw angels moving up and down and more faces along the steps. God would raise a leader from Esau's family. All the rulers of the nations who had hurt Jacob's people would give in to this leader. He would treat them harshly and rule over them with force. They wouldn't be able to stop him. Eventually, he would demand that people worship false gods and the dead. Many from Jacob's family would be handed over—some to this harsh ruler, and others to God's judgment.

Jacob, I want you to understand this: your descendants will one day live in a foreign land, where they will be treated badly and forced into slavery. They will be beaten and hurt daily. But the people who treat them this way will be judged by God. When the time comes and a king rises up and fights back, God will bring judgment to that place. Then your people, the children of Israel, will be freed from the power of those who ruled over them with cruelty. They will no longer be shamed or mocked by their enemies.

This king will be the one who brings justice and punishment to those who attacked Israel. At the end of this time, those who suffer will cry out, and the Lord will listen. He will feel compassion, and even the strongest will show pity because angels and archangels will pray for the rescue of your people. Women among your people will have many children again, and the Lord will fight for them.

The land of their enemies will suffer. Their food supplies will be empty, there will be no wine or fruit. The ground will be full of crawling creatures and other harmful things. There will be earthquakes and destruction. When God passes judgment on that land, He will lead your people out of slavery. They will be saved from the insults of their enemies.

The king who stood against them will face revenge. Even though he stood proudly, thinking he was powerful, the people cried out— and the Lord heard them. He poured out His anger on Leviathan, the sea monster, and struck down the wicked ruler named Thalkon with a sword because that ruler had lifted himself up against the true God.

Then, Jacob, your righteousness and that of your ancestors—and of your children who follow your path—will be seen. Your descendants will blow the trumpet, and the entire kingdom of Edom will be destroyed, along with the kings and people of Moab.

The dream you had about the angels going up and down the ladder points to something in the future. In the last days, someone will come from God. He will want to connect what is above with what is below. Before He arrives, your sons and daughters will speak messages from God, and young people will have visions of Him.

Strange and powerful signs will happen when He is about to come: a tree that is cut down will bleed, babies just a few months old will speak clearly, and a child still in the womb will announce His coming. A young man will seem wise like an old man. Then, the One who has long been expected will arrive, but no one will know exactly how He comes. When He appears, the earth will celebrate because heaven's glory has come down to it. What was once far above will now be close.

From your family, a royal leader will grow. He will rise up and destroy the power of evil. He will be a savior—not just for your people, but for the tired and broken among the other nations too. He will be like a cloud offering shade from the heat, covering the whole world. Without Him, the world would remain broken. He is the one who connects heaven and earth.

When He arrives, idols made of bronze, stone, and carved images will speak out for three days. They will tell wise people what is happening on the earth. And by a special star, those seeking Him will find their way. They will see Him walking on earth—this One whom even the angels cannot fully see in heaven.

Then, God Himself will appear in human form. He will be held in the arms of a regular person. He will bring new life to humankind. He will restore what was lost when Adam and Eve sinned. The lies and tricks of evil will be broken, and all false gods will fall down in shame because they were built on lies. They will no longer be able to rule or pretend to speak truth. Their power will be taken from them, and they will have no more honor.

The child who comes will take their strength away. He will fulfill the promise God made to Abraham. He will smooth out everything rough and bring peace. He will throw all wickedness into the deep sea and perform amazing miracles in both heaven and earth.

But this savior will be wounded—in the house of someone He loves. When He is hurt, the time of salvation and the end of all evil will be near. Those who hurt Him will be wounded in return, and their wound will never heal. But the One who was wounded will be worshiped by all creation. People from everywhere, including all nations, will place their hope in Him. Everyone who knows His name will never be ashamed. His strength and His life will never end.

Sefer Yetzirah
(The Book of Creation)

Introduction to The Book of Creation

The Book of Creation, also known as Sefer Yetzirah, is one of the oldest mystical texts in Jewish tradition. It describes how the universe began, explaining that creation happened through divine wisdom, the Hebrew alphabet, and ten powerful forces called the sefirot. These forces represent different aspects of divine energy shaping the world.

Even though the book is short and filled with mystery, it offers deep ideas about the connection between language, creation, and the divine. Its influence can be seen in later mystical teachings and philosophical ideas about the nature of existence. Including this text in the Apocrypha collection allows readers to explore one of the most fascinating and important discussions about creation in sacred literature.

Chapter 1

The mirror is not being charitable.

Even with all the noise downstairs—footsteps echoing and voices calling—I lock the door and face the mirror. The glass is covered in smudges and fingerprints, but I can still see myself clearly. I examine my face carefully, like a doctor studying a patient. It's familiar but frustrating.

The dim light doesn't do me any favors, but turning on the overhead lamp would be worse. Its bluish glow would make me look pale and sickly, like I had been pulled out of deep water. That's not the look I need. I have to seem calm, alert, and put together.

My eyes land on my hair—thin, straight, and already greasy, even though I washed it just an hour ago. My fingers reach for the small gray comb in my pocket. A few quick strokes would smooth it down, but I decide to wait until the last moment before leaving. I glance at my forehead—wide and high. Nili calls it "clever," but I never know if she's joking. The smirk on her face when she says it keeps me guessing. If I were as smart as I pretend to be, I wouldn't be in this mess.

Despite washing my face with strong, medicated soap, my forehead is already shiny again. The soap is pink and raw-looking, like uncooked meat, but it does nothing to stop my skin from gleaming. I wonder where all this oil comes from. Which part of me is betraying me? My thick, straight eyebrows arch slightly, as if they, too, are trying to figure it out. I skip over my eyes, unwilling to meet the expression I know is waiting there.

"Telma? Telma!" The doorknob rattles hard. It's Aunt Edith. She hates locked doors. She always needs to know what's going on in everyone's lives, and it makes me uneasy. The family still talks about the time her younger son put a lock on his bedroom door to keep her out. She hired a carpenter to take the whole door off. In response, he called her crazy and moved out. She told everyone that any son who locks her out has no place in her house. They've made up since then, and now she considers herself a parenting expert. I can't stand her.

"Leave me alone," I say, my voice flat but tired. She doesn't argue. Her hurried footsteps tell me she was never planning to push further. Aunt Edith knows when to stop—she's not stupid.

I wonder if it's a mistake to let her wander around the house, poking into things and gossiping. But some fights aren't worth having. Sometimes, it's easier to give in.

I shift my focus to my nose—small and delicate, but slightly crooked from an old injury. Beneath the skin, tiny pieces of bone shift when I touch them, making a faint rustling sound. In winter, when I blow my nose too hard, pale veins appear along the sides, and a dull pain spreads through it. The ache reminds me that the damage is permanent.

"Telma!" Nili calls from downstairs this time. I ignore her and keep staring at my slightly bent nose. The memory of how it happened still stings, and my cheeks flush. The sudden color makes me look oddly eager.

"You might want to hide this," Nili says from behind the door.

"Hide what?"

"You know." Her voice is teasing, making me rush to the door. "I'll just leave it here." She walks away—not because she respects my space, but because she doesn't want an argument. I open the door and pick up the small book she left. I catch my reflection in the mirror. I don't look happy.

It took a week for anyone to realize my nose was broken. The impact had been unbearable. I saw stars—real ones, not just a figure of speech—green and purple bursts exploding in my vision. I lay still, too humiliated to move, until the stars faded, and I dragged myself to the bathroom. When the water ran pink, I knew it was bad. But since my nose looked normal, I felt relieved.

"So typical," Simon had said later. "As long as it doesn't show on the outside, you don't care. You'd let yourself rot inside as long as you still look fine." He wasn't wrong. Even now, with everything inside me falling apart, I'm obsessed with keeping up appearances. And I think I'm managing.

The pain in my nose lasted all week, but I assumed it was just bruising. Then, Nili, always blunt, pointed out, "Your nose looks a little off to the left." That's when I was finally taken to the hospital. They put a cold, stiff white cast on it. For two weeks, I carried that weight on my face, clinging to the hope that when it came off, everything would be back to normal.

When the cast finally came off, I looked in the mirror and saw a nose that wasn't mine. Right in the middle sat a small, stubborn bump that hadn't been there before. The shock hit me like another punch. I screamed and argued, refusing to believe it, until they had to calm me down with an injection. They kept telling me it was just swelling, that my nose would go back to normal soon.

Of course, that never happened. Everyone insists my nose looks just as good as before, but I know the truth. That tiny bump wasn't invited, yet there it is, sitting in the center of my face for all to see. Simon, in his usual clueless way, once told me the bump wasn't on my nose—it was in my head. He couldn't be more wrong.

I look at my nose now and try to smile. But somehow, smiling makes the bump stand out even more, so I let my lips relax into their usual tight, pinched shape. They remind me of two little pink snails resting on my chin—one slightly plumper than the other, the top one always dry. Behind them sits my tongue, hidden but sharp, skilled in spinning lies. And today, I already know, will be a day full of them.

I stick my tongue out at the mirror in defiance. "You're such a liar," I say to my reflection. "A master at it. What would I do without you?" My voice drips with sarcasm, but beneath it, there's something close to admiration. Before I can sink any further into this strange moment, a knock at the door startles me. A sharp reminder that life outside this room is still moving, waiting impatiently.

"Telma, we don't have all day!" comes the frustrated voice from the other side. "Hurry up!"

But today isn't just another day, is it? It's different. How often does someone get a test like this—one with no hope, no expectations, no fear of disappointment? I stand in front of the mirror, more exposed than ever before, studying myself like a stranger looking through a microscope. My eyes follow every line and curve of my face.

There they are—my cheeks. Go on, Telma, really look at them. There's no one here to impress. Stop sucking them in.

And there it is, my little double chin, tucked away behind the "real one." Oh, Telma, what's going to happen to you with this round, moonlike face? I sigh, noticing the puffiness in my features. Is it from all the crying last night? Or the endless snacking afterward? All I know is that lifting my head off the pillow this morning felt impossible. As if everything I ate and felt yesterday had settled inside me, thick and heavy, clouding my mind.

I look beneath my eyes—those eyes I still can't meet properly in the mirror. Dark shadows rest there, like bruises that refuse to fade. My skin has taken on a dull, slightly greenish tint, like cheese left in the sun too long. For the first time ever, I feel too pale. Normally, I take pride in my light skin. In this sunny country, I go to great lengths to keep it that way. Few people understand the effort it takes.

Every time I step outside, it's a whole process: oversized sunglasses, a giant hat, and a loose men's shirt to block out the sun. My family—the same people now arguing downstairs as they rush to leave—thinks I'm being ridiculous. They don't know how creative I've become in avoiding the sun. Like that time I forgot my hat at

Nili's house and walked home with my head tilted forward, hair covering my face as a shield. I nearly got run over. The car skidded to a stop inches from my feet. The driver, wide-eyed and furious, jumped out to yell at me, but I barely heard him. My mind was somewhere else, picturing something much worse—my body sprawled on the pavement, arms and legs bent in awkward directions, my skin slowly darkening under the sun's harsh rays, like a chicken roasting in an oven.

Oh yes, my face is pale. Very, very pale.

I lower my eyes to my chest, noticing, as always, its slight unevenness. My left breast is just a little fuller, as if my heart is pressing against it from the inside, expanding with each slow beat. Ba-boom, ba-boom, ba-boom. Strange. I thought my heart would be racing today, but it's not. It's steady, unremarkable. I feel a faint tingling in my fingertips and glance at my hands. My hands. I've never liked them. They're small and stubby, with short nails because I can't stop picking at the skin around them. The tiny cuts sting when I touch them.

These hands—always moving, always restless. It's a shame they aren't beautiful, considering they're the part of me I see the most. Nili's hands, though—hers are beautiful. Truly beautiful.

The loud banging on the door snaps me out of my thoughts. This time, Aunt Edith isn't giving up. She pounds her fists against the wood, shouting, "We're all waiting for you! Only you! As always!"

Only you. The words sting, bringing back memories of past scoldings. Like the time I lost my lunchbox with my brand-new sunglasses inside, making everyone tear the house apart looking for it. Only you. Or when I stuck a lollipop in Simon's hair, delaying our trip to the countryside. Only you. And the day I threw up all over the cushions Aunt Edith had spent hours embroidering, making her complain that her eyes nearly fell out from all that stitching.

Yes, Telma. Always you.

But today isn't like those other days. Today, we are getting ready to bury Grandma Gerta. It's her funeral.

I finally lift my eyes to the mirror. My reflection stares back, my gaze a little too bright, holding something I can't quite hide. It almost looks like excitement, though I won't admit it—not even to myself.

Chapter 8

Grandma, what is this?
A book.
What kind of book?
A very special one.

The Book of Creation now sits on a dusty shelf in the attic, even dirtier than when I first laid eyes on it as a child. Every time it's opened, it seems to absorb something, growing grimier with use. But instead of wearing down, it only becomes stronger—like a body building muscle through exercise. Maybe, dearie, you could have used a little more exercise yourself. This book doesn't lose power when it's used. Instead, it draws from an endless source, growing more potent each time.

This small, ordinary-looking book has bound itself to me in ways I can't explain. It is built on the idea that letters—when connected—can create entire worlds and bring life into existence. Every word spoken, whether out of ignorance, cruelty, curiosity, or indifference, has weight. It brings something new into the world. Even a name, spoken aloud—Telma—has the power to stir something unseen but real.

To you, the idea of letters shaping reality seems obvious, almost natural. What surprises you isn't their power, but the fact that your fragile, breakable body can wield it. Words last longer than you ever will. They are sturdy, unshaken by time—unlike your weak ovaries that may never bear life. Aleph, yod, shin—man. Aleph, shin, heh— woman. Creation isn't about flesh and blood, about veins and vessels pumping inside you. It is something deeper, more fundamental.

I remember the first time I held the book. A jolt ran through me, like my hands had turned into beams of light. It felt alive, as if I was clutching a tiny, trembling animal—something delicate but powerful, like a kitten with bones as light as air beneath soft fur. It was pure hunger. A raw, desperate need.

I wouldn't let go. Grandma Gerta had to pry the book from my hands. My fingers clenched so tightly that when she finally pulled it away, I was filled with rage. I slapped her. A red mark, shaped like my small fingers, bloomed on her cheek. But she didn't get mad. She didn't even flinch. She just rubbed her face, slowly, knowingly, like she had been expecting this. Like she understood.

I begged her to let me read it. I asked again and again. Each time, she just smiled. But it wasn't her usual smile—it was something different. Something strange, almost affectionate. Her gray-green eyes sparkled like jewels hidden deep beneath the sea. Eyes just like mine.

"Now can I read it?" I would ask.
"Not yet."
"But I'm in third grade now."
"Not yet, kindeleh."
"Then when?"
"You'll know."

Now my eyes are dry, wide open. My mind is sharp, clear, logical. I don't trust anyone—not even myself. I have no patience for people who drift through life like ghosts, their hands always trembling, their voices soft and uncertain. I prefer those who keep their feet firmly planted, even if the ground beneath them is poisoned. People who see the world for what it really is—ugly, cruel, unkind—and do not turn away.

I don't believe in stories or promises. I don't trust words, looks, or even scents. They can all deceive. And I have been deceived too many times, especially by those I once loved.

I am a skeptic. A pessimist. A person who dislikes herself as much as she dislikes others. My disappointment in humanity runs so deep that it has forced my mind open to something else. Something more. There are forces at work beyond what humans can understand, and I feel them moving in the world around me. When I walk through crowded streets, the air hums with something invisible, something living. The rhythm shifts—sometimes slow, sometimes fast. The sun sinks, the sky burns with streaks of gold and fire, and for a moment, everything feels thin, exposed, alive.

I know there are languages beyond words. And you do, too, liar. You talk so fast, tripping over your own tongue, always racing to finish before someone else can cut in. You move quicker than your heart, quicker than your thoughts.

Here I am, locked in my room, tears streaming down my face—thick, cloudy, impossible to hold back. Everyone says Telma is growing up. But TelmaChild has no breasts, no blood, no soft fuzz on her body. She is not a woman. Only an empty, aching space that cannot be filled.

She is small. Round. Trapped in a body that refuses to change, living in a world just slightly off from this one—a world with its own rules, its own unbreakable laws. Under her pillow, she hides a small book, its pages worn thin from use. She sleeps with it close, curled around it as if it is a part of her.

And in her dreams, a single image repeats, again and again. She wakes knowing it is not a dream. But it is not reality, either.

What it is, she cannot say.

In my dream, he stands with his back to me, a dark figure against a world swallowed by flames. Thick smoke fills the air, burning my throat, making it hard to breathe. My lungs tighten, my breath comes in short gasps, and the unbearable heat of destruction surrounds us. But his hands reach for me, gripping tightly, lifting me above the burning ground. The scent of charred wood and the distant sound of collapsing buildings grow louder. His lips meet mine—warm, parted, burning. The air is pulled from my body. My throat tightens. My mouth is dry. Our lips press together, hot and consuming. A kiss. The kiss.

Ash drifts in the smoky air, tiny embers floating around us. My tongue stings—it feels raw, like a scorched, useless thing. He turns, and I slip from his grasp. A building crashes to the ground behind him. His eyes squeeze shut, empty and unreadable.

I wake up suddenly, heart pounding. The house is silent except for the faint creak of footsteps. From the kitchen, I hear my father muttering to himself as he paces across the tiled floor. Shadows stretch along the hallway walls. If this were Grandma's house, I would have wet the bed in fear. Again.

The morning after the pipes burst, the house was eerily quiet. The panic had faded, replaced by something heavier, something unspoken.

"I don't know what caused it," said the plumber Uncle Avrum called in. He held a giant, rust-covered wrench and wiped his boots on the doormat, leaving dark smudges behind.

"I missed all the excitement last night," Nili said, smiling in a way that made my stomach drop. Her tone was too casual. My voice came out dry and rough when I finally spoke.

"What do you mean?" I asked, hoping she was only talking about the pipes.

"Simon seemed pretty shaken up about what happened," she said lightly, as if it didn't matter. I clenched my jaw and said nothing. I refused to let her see how much those words unsettled me, refused to let her glimpse even a fraction of my shame.

"Enough!" Aunt Tzilla's sharp voice cut through the air, startling both of us. Her face was pale, her expression cold and unreadable. She turned her gaze on me. "Have you called Schreiber yet?"

"No. Not yet." I hadn't found the strength to deal with whatever the lawyer had to say.

As I walked through the house, I felt tiny bits of dirt falling from my skin. I hadn't showered since the pipes broke. The dust clung to me like armor, a barrier between me and the world. I wanted to stay this way, wrapped in the filth, until it hardened and cracked on its own, revealing the softer, vulnerable skin beneath. But, of course, that wasn't possible. The eyes around me saw straight through it. They always did.

Schreiber's office was cold, sleek, too polished. Chrome and glass everywhere. Mother and I sank into the deep leather chairs, feeling out of place, feeling dirty. Every tiny movement we made seemed to emphasize how little we belonged here. The secretary approached, as put-together as the office itself. She wore a pale blue angora sweater that hugged her body, matching her soft-colored shoes.

"Can I get you something to drink?" she asked, her voice too smooth, too practiced.

"Coffee," I said flatly. "Three sugars, lots of milk." I watched the slight movement of her sweater as she turned.

"And for you?" she asked, looking at my mother.

"Nothing," Mother whispered, barely making a sound, as if the chair itself was swallowing her whole.

"She'll have coffee too," I snapped, annoyed by the secretary's effortless poise, by the perfect way her life seemed to fit together. I imagined her tangled up with Schreiber on his desk, their sweat mixing with the scattered papers. The thought made my stomach turn.

Schreiber sat across from us, dressed in an angora sweater of his own—maybe a matching set. His voice was smooth, distant, the tone of a man who had dealt with far too many cases like ours.

"Mrs. Sander left a rather unusual condition in her will," he said, his eyes flicking to my mother for a brief moment, as if hinting at the disappointments to come. We already knew the truth—there wasn't much money left.

"She split her bank accounts between her two daughters," he continued, pausing for effect.

"But the apartment on Maharal Street," I interrupted, already knowing what he was going to say, "she left it to me."

Schreiber studied me, his eyes narrowing slightly. "There is a condition," he said, motioning to the secretary. She reappeared, balancing two steaming mugs of coffee on a tray.

"I know what the condition is," I said, keeping my voice steady.

"You do?" Mother's eyes widened, her shock barely contained. I could already see the panic building in her, the realization of what this meant. Aunt Tzilla would be furious. The rich never take it well when something they think belongs to them is taken away. On the way home, Mother would wail in the car, dabbing at her face with a crumpled tissue. But for now, she just stared at me like I was something unfamiliar—something rare and unexpected. Lucky. That was the word running through her mind. She looked at me as if I had somehow become special.

What a fool she was.

"I have to move in," I said calmly. "Right after the seven days of mourning are over. And I have to live there alone. Isn't that right?"

Schreiber hesitated only for a second before nodding. "Yes, that's the main requirement." His voice remained smooth, neutral. He picked up his glass of water and took a slow sip, his movements clean, measured, practiced. Everything about him was careful, controlled. It almost made me like him—despite the sweater, despite the secretary, or maybe even because of them.

"And what if I say no?" I asked, though I already knew the answer. Beside me, Mother tensed, her breath hitching.

But I didn't need Schreiber to respond. There was no room for refusal. No loophole in the will. Just like there was no mention of the real inheritance my grandmother had left me—the one hidden away in the attic. Small, tattered, waiting for me.

On the way home, Mother's awe turned into irritation. She glared at me, her excitement fading into quiet resentment. She hated conflict. So did I, if I was being honest. In that way, we were alike. But that similarity meant nothing now.

Because one thing was certain.

I was going to live in Grandma Gerta's house.

I was going to take her place.

Chapter 12

The white tablecloth is stained with wine, its surface blotchy and smeared like an old bandage. Passover Seder doesn't feel like a celebration—it feels like a battlefield, filled with spilled wine and simmering resentment.

I pour myself another glass, letting the deep red liquid flood my body, dulling the sharp edges of my thoughts. It's the only way to survive this long, suffocating night of endless rituals and restless hours.

Why is this night different from all other nights? The familiar words ring out across the table. How, indeed? What makes this night different? Bitter matzo? Sharp, lingering fear? Unspoken tensions? A metallic taste lingers in my mouth, a mix of wine and something sharper, something almost like blood. Drink, Telma. Drink more. You haven't had enough yet. Your mind is still too clear. You can still see through their masks.

I look around at faces so much like my own, chewing matzo balls, dribbling greasy broth onto their chins. A room full of people pretending this night is sacred, as if they're anything other than a tangled mess of history, obligation, and quiet contempt.

And yet, look who's judging.

The dirt on my skin, the grime beneath my nails—it's my armor.

I let it settle into me, let it hide beneath my crisp white holiday blouse. If someone planted a field of potatoes around my collar, they'd probably grow. Later, when I peel this blouse off, the inside will be speckled with tiny brown spots of sweat and dust, proof of everything I try to bury.

I stare at the jagged piece of matzo in my hand. Its uneven surface is dotted with dark spots. Just burn marks from the oven? Or something else? The old whispers creep into my mind, the accusations, the horrifying stories passed down in secret. Could it be true? Could we be capable of such things? I scan the faces at the table, wondering how many of them would hesitate before picking up a knife. Not many. Maybe not even me.

I take a bite. The edges scrape against my tongue, rough and unyielding. My mouth fills with that bitter, metallic taste again. I swallow.

Something is here. Watching. Waiting. It's been here all along, hiding in the cracks of the ceramic casserole dish at the center of the table or clinging to the walls of my chest. I don't know where, but I can feel it.

We sit stiffly, dressed in our best clothes, surrounding a table heavy with food and tension. We sing the songs, just as we're supposed to: Why on this night do we eat only bitter herbs? Generations of self-loathing Jews like me have sung this same song, sitting at tables just like this one, surrounded by people who claim to be family. No night exposes the weight of family obligations like Passover, where every word spoken, every forced smile, adds to the unspoken debts we pretend not to owe each other.

I glance around the table at the familiar faces. What ties me to these people? Mother. Father. Aunt Tzilla. Uncle Avrum. Nili. Simon.

Simon's distant parents. His clueless brother and his scheming wife, along with their three sticky-fingered children. Just listing them in my mind exhausts me.

The men recline in their chairs as tradition dictates, leaning into the pristine white pillows that make Aunt Tzilla's living room feel strangely like a brothel rather than a place of worship. Father's pillow is limp, barely filled, while Uncle Avrum's is thick and luxurious. Even tonight, a night supposedly about freedom, the hierarchy remains clear.

At the center of the table, the roasted chicken leg sits blackened and shriveled, resembling the charred limb of a child. My stomach turns. I swallow another gulp of wine to push down the nausea.

The hagaddah in my hands offers no comfort. A red-haired Moses glares at me from the pages, his cartoonish face twisted with fury. Beside him, massive waves rise, swallowing tiny, screaming figures whole. Later tonight, I know their faces will follow me into my dreams. Every holiday drags ghosts of past celebrations behind it, trapping me in an endless cycle. No matter how old I get, I'm still just a shadow of my younger self.

Another glass of wine is poured. Drink it, Telma. Drink until the emptiness inside you overflows. Maybe the fear will fade. I force it down, wincing. Across the table, Nili watches me, her lips curling into a knowing smile. She sits beside Simon in the chair that used to be mine, comfortable in the space I once occupied. She thinks she's won.

I am nothing but a little girl who has, once again, lost the afikoman prize.

"For finding the afikoman this year, little Telma, what would you like as your reward?"

Father leans toward me, his voice filled with both pride and uncertainty. He isn't used to leading these gatherings, to playing the role of the patriarch.

I look at him, but all I can think about is how easily I've been replaced. By Nili. By Simon's family. By everyone.

"I want a red scooter," I say quietly, already bracing for the disappointment that always follows.

"No problem," Father replies, too eager, too proud. "Whatever you want, you'll get."

There's something new in his eyes—a rare moment where he seems to like himself, to enjoy playing the generous father.

He starts the traditional search for the afikoman, lifting pillows, peeking behind plates, but we all know he won't find it. That's the unspoken rule of Passover: parents aren't supposed to find it, no matter how carelessly it's hidden. It's a ritual. A game that lets children hold a small, temporary power over the adults. Without it, their natural urge to steal or hide would show up in far worse ways.

I think of the times I stole coins from Mother's old, faded purse.

And then, the impossible happens.

Father finds it.

He lifts the napkin-wrapped matzo, holding it in his hands like something foreign, something wrong. He doesn't move. He doesn't speak. He just stands there in the middle of the room, and if I had been paying closer attention, I would have noticed how badly his hands were shaking.

The tears don't come right away. I am still gathering air, my small chest rising, preparing for the wail that will follow. My eyes are wide, my braids framing a face frozen in confusion.

Across the table, Aunt Tzilla watches Father with quiet disgust.

Nili, already pleased with the fancy makeup kit she received as her prize, giggles softly.

Mother leans toward Father, her whisper like a blade slicing through the air. "Oh, Reuven," she hisses, disappointment dripping from every syllable.

And then, at last, the sobs break free.

Tears pour down my hot cheeks as I cry, my voice trembling with betrayal.

"Why did you find it, Daddy? Why? Yucky Daddy!"

My dream of a red scooter crumbles, replaced by something far worse: the realization that my own father has let me down.

He doesn't move. He just stands there, holding the afikoman like it has turned to dust in his hands. If I weren't blinded by my own tears, I might have noticed the way his face changed—the regret settling in, the quiet shame. He hadn't meant to find it. He only wanted, for once, to be the hero. To feel like a winner, even if just for a moment.

The red scooter was bought. It sat in the corner of the living room, bright and untouched, like a monument to that night. The first time I rode it, I fell hard, scraping my ankle so badly that blood spilled onto the pavement, pooling like some kind of strange offering. After that, I refused to ride it again. It stayed there for years, covered in dust, a silent reminder of something I didn't want to think about.

Why on this night do we eat only bitter herbs? The words echo in my mind, their melody turning into something cruel. A reminder of just how deep the bitterness really goes.

I drop my gaze to the hagaddah in my lap. The letters blur, and I'm grateful for it. This night will be easier to get through if I don't have to see the words. I've had enough of words—the ones in this book, the ones in the forbidden book I hid away, the ones I never dared to read aloud. They all have too much power over me.

Moses stares at me from the page, his red hair flaming with righteous anger. His cartoonish face twists in accusation. Look at yourself, he seems to say. Drunk at the Seder table. Is this how a proper Jewish girl behaves? As if your other sins weren't enough, now you have to add this to the list?

"Sssimon," I slur, my tongue slow and heavy in my mouth. "That's a beautiful sssshirt." I drag out the words, letting them hang in the air, watching them land. There's no point pretending anymore. Once everyone realizes how drunk you are, the need to keep up appearances disappears. And with that, at least, comes a little relief.

"I picked it out for him," Nili cuts in smoothly, her voice filled with pride. "We went shopping yesterday, and I told him we weren't leaving without that navy blue shirt. It's perfect for him—it really makes his eyes stand out."

No one flinches at her casual use of we. Aunt Tzilla and Uncle Avrum lean in, interested, eager for more details about this new connection. Simon's parents, Manny and Batya, don't notice anything at all. They're too busy shoveling food into their mouths, fat glistening on their chins, pooling beneath their skin with each greedy bite. Mother sits quietly, picking at her stuffed chicken, digging into it as though it's done something to offend her. She won't look at me. But her hands keep moving, tearing at the lifeless bird, pulling it apart piece by piece. She knows what's happening. She just refuses to acknowledge it.

Father sits beside her, gnawing on a bone, his face turned away. He won't look at me either.

"So, Telma," Uncle Avrum says, his voice dripping with fake interest, his shirt stained with gravy. "What's going on with you these days? You're thirty now, right? Don't you have a nice young man yet?"

No, Uncle Avrum, there is no "nice young man." I don't want someone nice. I want someone messy, someone whose soul is dark and tangled, someone who understands the chaos inside my head. I want—

If I wanted to, I could stretch my foot under the table, let it brush against Simon's leg. He's sitting right across from me, chewing methodically, his jaw working like a machine. For the first time, I really look at him—at the way he eats, at the way his body glistens with sweat, at the almost animalistic way he consumes everything in front of him.

Seder night turns us all into something less than human.

I glance under the table, half-expecting to see my legs ending in hooves.

"I'm doing just fine, Avrum," I finally say, forcing a tight smile. The wine hasn't loosened my tongue enough to say what I really think, to tell him to drown himself in a bathtub. Those words stay locked inside, like so many others.

Aunt Tzilla's voice cuts through the air, sharp and laced with amusement. "Maybe things will be easier for you now," she says, her earrings catching the light. I notice for the first time how heavy they are, how they pull at her earlobes, dragging them downward. "You've got your own apartment now, don't you? Seems like a good deal for some lucky young man."

I feel my face heat up. The entire room flushes red—anger, embarrassment, and something else I can't quite name.

"What's with that look?" she presses. "Come on, you have to admit—it's a great deal for you. And honestly, you need it more than Nili does. Maybe that's why my mother left it to you."

What does she know about Grandma Gerta's wishes? Nothing. Absolutely nothing. But they hang in the air, invisible but heavy, waiting for someone to say them out loud.

I keep my face blank, my eyes fixed straight ahead. My mother looks small, defeated, her shoulders slumped like the weight of this conversation has crushed her. My father is no better—his eyes flicker nervously between Nili and Simon, but he says nothing. Neither of them does. Maybe they want to. Maybe they don't know how. Maybe it's easier to stay quiet. Either way, their silence says more than words ever could. Why couldn't they be different?

Their weakness drains me, pulling at whatever strength I have left. When the blood is weak, the soul is weak too.

I feel exposed, drowning in my own frustration. My body doesn't feel like my own—my breasts too firm, my hair too long, my skin prickling with discomfort. I hate this moment. It's like the part of the hagaddah I always get stuck reading, the passage filled with words that make my stomach twist. Somehow, every year, it lands on me, forcing me to read aloud the most embarrassing lines. It's like peeling back my own skin, layer by layer, leaving me raw and open.

Words like blood, menstruation, pubic hair—they come tumbling out, each one slicing through me, forcing me to put every awkward, shameful part of myself on display.

"Look, Mother, I have hair down there!" I had once said, young and naive, only to be met with her disgusted reply: "Don't act like a pig!"

But I am a pig. A small, foolish pig. And tonight, my afikomen burns in an invisible fire. I feel wrong, incomplete—like a woman who has waited too long for something she can't even name.

At the center of the table, Elijah's cup sits untouched, gleaming silver, almost sacred. I can't look away. What would happen if I drank from it? Would Elijah appear in a flash of light, furious at my disrespect? Or would nothing happen at all, except for the looks of horror on everyone's faces?

I'm tired of these rituals. Tired of this night that repeats itself year after year. Why do we keep coming back to this table, saying the same words, pouring wine into a cup that no one will ever drink from? My skin itches with tension, my whole body coiled tight like a spring. And then, before I even realize what I'm doing, I stand up.

I reach for Elijah's cup.

"Cheers!" I announce, my voice ringing in the silence.

Every head turns. Simon and Nili freeze. Aunt Tzilla's mouth falls open. My father, mid-bite, chokes on a tiny bone.

"To Grandma Gerta!" I say, louder now. "To the great freedom fighter who led the Warsaw Ghetto Uprising fifty years ago today! To Gerta!" The words tumble out faster. "To Gerta!" And before anyone can stop me, I tilt the cup back and drain it in one gulp.

The wine burns as it slides down my throat, but at least it doesn't taste like blood.

The silence is suffocating. They stare at me, horrified, their mouths slightly open, as if I've broken some unspoken law. They look like fish gasping for air, wide-eyed and wordless. In their eyes, I've confirmed every low expectation they've ever had of me.

I keep drinking as the night drags on, trying to drown the strange feeling rising inside me. But what am I waiting for? I don't even know.

I stumble into the kitchen. The countertops, wrapped in tin foil for Passover, glint under the harsh light, making the whole room look cold and sterile, like a morgue. I turn on the faucet, letting the water run over my hands, as if I can wash away the tension. But some things don't come clean.

A voice inside me whispers, Turn around.

And I do.

Through the open door, I see them—Nili and Simon—standing together on the tiny balcony.

They're close. Too close.

Simon's voice is hesitant. "I don't know if we should be doing this."

But Nili touches his arm, tilts her head toward him. Under the streetlight, their figures fit together perfectly, like the couple on a greeting card. And then, just like that, they kiss.

Slow. Deep. Real.

I don't move. The wine doesn't blur it. I see everything. My hands clench into fists, but I can't look away. It's beautiful. The most perfect kiss I've ever seen.

But it's not mine.

And just like that, something inside me snaps.

A wave of nausea hits, and suddenly, everything I've eaten and drunk comes rushing up. Matzo balls, sweet carrots, horseradish, wine—it all surges out, splattering onto the kitchen floor. Onto Nili's dress.

The mess clings to her like an accusation.

I collapse, shaking, too stunned to care.

Aunt Tzilla runs in, screaming about her ruined kitchen. My mother looks at me, silent, disappointed. Then, as always, she turns away.

I stay on the floor, covered in filth, feeling nothing.

But then, slowly, I push myself up.

I am not dead. Not yet.

Anyone who can pretend, who can keep playing the game, isn't truly gone.

I stumble out of the house, past the staring eyes, past Simon, who won't even look at me. I step into the night. The tears don't come. They harden inside me into something else.

I run.

I know exactly where I'm going.

And this time, I'm ready.

Chapter 13

The soil in the cemetery is dark and heavy. Above, a blood-red moon hangs in the sky.

You move with purpose, your entire body focused on what must be done. Every part of you feels alert, buzzing with anticipation. Your chest tightens, your skin tingles. Faster, Telma. Move faster. Your thighs brush together as you push forward.

You are completely clean. You spent the afternoon scrubbing yourself, making sure no trace of dirt remained. You scrubbed everywhere, but you paid special attention to that secret, delicate place between your legs—the hidden part of you, soft and red, always kept out of sight.

Move, now! You break into a run. Every step feels urgent, every second precious. In the distance, buildings crumble, sending sparks flying dangerously close. Laughter echoes from the darkness, sharp and familiar. The voices taunt you, their sing-song words floating through the night:

From earth and blood you knead the dough

Watch until it rises so...

You ignore them. There's no time for their nonsense. You dig your fingers into the soil, clawing at the ground, your nails cracking against the hardened dirt. Faster, Telma. They're coming. You can feel them getting closer. The sharp smell of smoke stings your nose, burns your throat. The earth resists, but you push on, dragging water from the basin near the purification room. The water runs pink, stained with something old, something powerful.

With steady hands, you shape him from the damp soil. Every curve, every line—you know them all. You've seen him before, in your mind, in your dreams. There is no room for mistakes. Not this time.

From earth and blood you knead the dough

Watch until it rises so...

The rhyme lingers, but you block it out. Your hands move on their own, driven by something deeper than thought. Maybe it's the lifeless body before you, calling you forward. Maybe it's the force inside you, pulling both of you toward something unstoppable.

Your fingers mold the shape of his shoulders, the curve of his neck, the broadness of his chest, the strength of his thighs. His body is smooth, powerful, strong—even though he is still only earth. But you know exactly what he must become, and you shape him without hesitation. Every motion feels like destiny, as if you've always known how to do this.

When you finally step back, he lies still on the ground. His quiet presence pulls you in. He looks peaceful, lost in a deep sleep. He has no idea what's coming. Neither do you. Not really. But your breath quickens as a memory flashes through your mind—the heat of a kiss, the way it drowned you, swallowed you whole. The thought almost breaks your focus, but you push it aside.

There is still more to do. And this time, you are sure of yourself.

You no longer wear the wedding dress. You know now that it was never the key to success. You are no one's bride. Not yet.

You begin to move, stepping carefully around him, tracing a perfect circle in the dirt. Once. Twice. Seven times. Your feet stay firm, your body steady. The words flow easily from your lips, etched into you like fire. Each sound carries power, each syllable feels alive. Beneath you, his body begins to glow. At first, it's only faint, like an ember catching light. Then, the glow deepens, as if breath is filling his form.

You don't stop. You keep circling. Seven more times. The air thickens, charged with energy. The world feels like it's waiting, holding its breath.

Then, the final moment arrives.

You lean over him, your lips forming the sacred word—the Name of Names, the word that seals creation.

Your mouth is dry, cracked from the force of your voice, but you don't stop. He is balanced on the edge of existence, and with this final act, everything will change.

You want this. You need this.

His body begins to shift. Water seeps into the earth, steaming and hissing, surrounding him in a mist. It looks like he might disappear into smoke, but you don't let it distract you. Your feet keep moving, circling again and again. The dizziness threatens to take over, but you push through it. Fool! you scream at yourself. Just this once, do something right!

Then, you see it.

Dark hair begins to spread over his body—thick, strong, alive. Fingernails and toenails emerge from the skin, twenty perfect crescents, gleaming in the dim light. They are flawless, whole, real.

And they move.

"Focus," you whisper to yourself, barely making a sound, afraid that even the smallest noise might break the delicate moment. Just a little longer. You're almost there.

Around you, the letters swirl like a raging storm, shifting, pulsing, alive with purpose. A large, rotting peach floats nearby, its sickly-sweet scent filling your nose, making your stomach turn. The two-headed child watches again, its teary, haunting eyes cutting through your concentration. In your hand, the small slip of paper shakes, almost burning through the bag that held it. Was this how it happened for her? Was this how Grandma Gerta did it all those years ago?

The thought flickers for only a second before you push it away. There's no time for doubt.

Carefully, you remove the sacred parchment and slip it into the mouth you shaped with such precision.

The lips tremble as the paper disappears inside. Full, perfect lips— so pure, so untainted. Could something so flawless ever tell a lie? But you don't let yourself wonder. Not now. You steady yourself and begin to recite the words again, each syllable slow and deliberate. You know that one wrong sound could ruin everything.

A faint noise—wet, raw, almost like the first gasp of a newborn— breaks the silence. The final piece has fallen into place. You lean in, your voice barely above a whisper:

"And He breathed into his nostrils the breath of life, and man became a living soul."

And then, you wait.

Waiting has become part of you, as natural as breathing. You know it well. It is woven into the deepest parts of your being.

He lies before you, still and smooth, his lips sealed. Nothing happens. The air grows thick with the weight of failure. You start to accept the inevitable—that you are alone, that you were always meant to be alone.

Your knees give out, and you sink to the ground. There are no tears. Even that would be too much effort. You press your face into the dirt, letting its coolness offer whatever comfort it can. You will stay here until you disappear, until the last bit of hope inside you is swallowed by the earth.

And then—you hear it.

Faint. Subtle.

A heartbeat.

Your lips, still buried in the dirt, rest against his chest. The warmth spreads beneath you. Alive. You lift your head in shock. His chest rises and falls. His heartbeat grows steadier, stronger. He breathes.

Your own heart pounds in response.

Then, he moves.

His limbs tremble, his eyes flutter open—dark and rich, the color of the soil itself. His gaze meets yours, and for a moment, something flickers in them before vanishing. He stretches his arms, shifts his body, his movements slow but full of power. And then, he stands.

Towering over you.

The golem has risen. The man you created with your own hands, shaped by your own will.

You push yourself to your feet, tilting your head back to meet his eyes. The moon is gone now, swallowed by the night.

This is the moment. You must name him.

You take a breath, steadying yourself. The name has been inside you all along, waiting for this very moment. Every letter must be right—every sound must fit the body you brought into being. A mistake would leave him incomplete, broken. And after all this, you refuse to accept anything less than perfection.

Your lips part. They are dry, trembling.

You swallow. And then, you speak.

"Saul."

The name barely leaves your lips, yet it carries weight.

Saul—the borrowed one. The man who is not yours to keep.

His eyes lock onto yours. And you know—he understands.

The streets are eerily quiet. The night feels darker than ever. It is almost as if fate has cleared the way, ensuring that no one is there to see you lead this towering, naked form toward home. You wrap him in an old tarp, found behind the purification room, and together you walk through the empty streets.

The air is thick with the scent of citrus—blooming orange trees mixed with the sweetness of rotting peaches. The wild fragrance of flowers fills the silence. Saul pauses, his eyes wide, drinking in the world as if seeing it for the first time. You catch his expression and feel something strange rise inside you.

You smile.

But just as you reach the entrance of your building, something catches your eye.

A lifeless bird.

Its gray feathers are tangled with red, its small body broken, its beak frozen open in an eternal, silent cry.

You stop.

A chill runs through you.

The night feels heavier now, pressing down with the weight of creation—and the weight of what comes next.

Chapter 14

The apartment feels strangely alive, like it's holding its breath. My eyes drift around the room, stopping on the old wooden dresser from Warsaw, the towering stack of religious books, the heavy rug covered in dust, the embroidered fawn trapped behind a glass frame. Everything is still, quiet, as if waiting.

I did it. My body is tense, my eyes bright, like a kid suddenly taken seriously as an adult. I stand in the middle of this dingy room, taking in the drooping plants and the sticky floor covered in smudged fingerprints. Crumbs roll across the ground—leftovers from some forgotten snack. This place is a mess. How could anyone visit here? And yet, I'm not alone. Someone else is watching, his eyes scanning the room. Will this be his home one day? His face gives nothing away, blank and unreadable. But then, his gaze shifts—upward, toward the attic. There's something sharp in his expression, something questioning. He sees more than I expected. I look away, embarrassed. My pride, my guilt, my uncertainty—it's all mixed up inside me, swirling between fear and hope.

But still, I did it. Somehow, I actually made this happen.

The air between us feels heavy. He's standing so close now that I take a step back without thinking. He's tall, solid, like a statue come to life. His deep brown eyes roam over my pale skin, searching for something. I don't know what. And whatever it is, he doesn't seem to find it. He just waits. His eyelashes are so perfect, they look like they were sewn on by hand.

But wasn't I the one who made him?

The thought won't leave my head. Me, me, me. I built him with my own hands. He's here, breathing, moving, because of me. I want him to scoop me up, to lift me off the ground.

But he doesn't.

We just stand there, waiting, caught in the same silent moment.

Memories rush back—me and Simon, running to the cemetery the night after Grandma Gerta died.

"You'll see," I had told him, buzzing with confidence. "It's going to work this time. Just wait."

"What if it comes alive and attacks us?" Simon's voice had shaken. "They say golems are unbelievably strong, and they always end up in violent situations. What if it's angry that we brought it to life without asking?"

His fear had been real. And, honestly, it was no surprise we failed that night. Fear always kills creation. Always.

But me? Was I fearless?

"You don't get it," I told him, practically shaking with excitement. "The best part about making a golem is that we control everything. It doesn't move or even blink unless we tell it to. That's what makes it so amazing."

What a fool I was.

Now, the last thing I want to do is give orders. I don't know how. The only commands I've ever given are to my parents—"Open the window!" or "Move, that's my seat!" or "Where's my gray skirt?" Everyone else? I only order them around in my head. Trip and fall. Disappear. Burn in hell. But, of course, no one ever listens.

And him? I can't do it. I won't. What would I even say?

His stare doesn't waver, challenging me. "Go on," his eyes seem to say. "Give me a command."

"Umm… uh… go to the kitchen," I mumble, barely above a whisper.

Will he listen?

His body shifts, his movements smoother now, no longer stiff like before. He walks through the parlor with ease, stopping by the sink, like he's been here before. And that's when I realize—I didn't need to tell him where to go. He already knew.

A hundred questions flood my mind, but I push them aside. Instead, I follow him, drawn toward the stove, feeling the sudden urge to cook for him.

What a fool I am.

The dining table is set with the fancy china—the ones with red flowers that look like fresh wounds. I'm nowhere near as good at cooking as Nili, so I keep it simple. Slices of oranges and peaches, uneven from my clumsy hands. Matzos, sharp-edged and brittle, like something ready for battle.

He stands motionless by the sink, in the exact spot where I once stood kissing Simon. The memory feels distant, unimportant—like something out of an old book. On this date, in this apartment, such-and-such happened. But who cares? What does it matter now? Simon barely reached the spice rack. Saul, though—his head nearly touches the tallest cupboard.

I'm glad I used so much dirt. If you're going to create something, you should do it properly. I remember the effort—digging, scraping, shaping. My hands still ache from it, my broken nails stinging from the dirt trapped underneath. Saul's dark eyes drop to my hands, noticing. I quickly brush them clean, letting the dirt fall to the floor.

His body flinches, just barely, at the sound. His face stays unreadable.

Why isn't he sitting? The realization sinks in, draining me. I say the word, "Sit," and he does. No hesitation. The huge figure lowers himself into the chair, but his gaze stays locked on my hands, like he's waiting for me to tell him to pick up the fallen dirt.

I don't. Not yet.

I grab a peach and bite into it, the soft flesh giving way beneath my teeth. My stomach twists, unsure if I'm hungry or just anxious. Saul doesn't move. His eyes follow the pink juice running down my chin. He does nothing to help. Nothing at all.

"Eat," I whisper, urging him.

Still, he doesn't move.

Frustrated, I cut a small piece of peach and place it in his hand. He stares at it, his expression shifting—was that sadness? "It's really good," I say, trying to encourage him. "Go ahead, eat." But he doesn't.

I try again, this time using a fork to lift a slice to his lips. But when I press it against his mouth, he doesn't open. His teeth don't budge. Then I remember—there's a slip of paper under his tongue, the thing that holds his essence. A cold fear grips me. What if the paper gets damaged? What if he collapses right here, turning into nothing but a pile of dirt on my kitchen floor? My hand freezes, and the peach slice slips from the fork, rolling down his chest and leaving a sticky trail.

His eyes flicker with something like impatience.

I know offering him coffee is pointless. Instead, I sit across from him, sipping my lukewarm drink in silence. Our so-called meal sits untouched—dried-out peach slices, bits of dirt scattered on the table, old photographs smudged with stains. These ordinary things remind me of my failure. The kitchen feels too quiet, the air too heavy. And then I notice something strange—the birds outside are silent. Their absence gnaws at me, but I shove the thought aside. Not now, Telma. Focus.

I clear the table without asking for help, feeling ridiculous. What kind of person creates a golem only to end up serving him? At this rate, I'll be the one with a slip of paper under my tongue, another mindless servant, another cliché. The thought makes my stomach turn. I bump the table with my foot, spilling coffee all over both of us.

Saul moves instantly. He stands so fast that the table crashes against the wall. Plates shatter, photographs flutter to the floor, and oranges roll across the tiles, bursting and leaking juice. He backs away, pressing himself into a corner, his face frozen in shock as he watches the coffee drip.

I follow his gaze and see it—a small hole forming in his skin where the liquid touched. It's dark and muddy, the edges crumbling.

Panic grips me. I ruined him.

The hole spreads, oozing black sludge. Saul doesn't move, doesn't try to stop it. His wide, trusting eyes beg me for help. I step forward, but as soon as my fingers brush the wound, he jerks back violently, almost knocking me over. He looks at me with unbearable pain, his body trembling. The wound keeps growing, and the sharp smell of damp earth fills the room.

Desperate, I grab a dying houseplant, scooping up its dry soil. Without thinking, I press the dirt into the wound. The moment it touches his skin, it absorbs, sealing the hole.

I let out a shaky breath. It worked.

Saul takes my hand and places it over the spot where the hole had been. His eyes shine with something close to gratitude, and suddenly, I feel ashamed.

What now? The night isn't over, and I still don't know what to do with him. He's a stranger in my home. Where will he sleep? Should I let him into my bed? The thought makes my chest tighten. I don't like sharing my space, and the few times I have, it ended badly.

I hesitate, unsure. What am I supposed to say? What am I

supposed to do? I stand there, frozen, overwhelmed by my own choices.

Then, as if he can hear my thoughts, Saul turns and walks toward the attic. I don't stop him. I just watch as his tall, solid figure moves away. I imagine him standing there every night, keeping silent watch while I toss and turn in Grandma Gerta's massive, empty bed. Maybe this is how it's meant to be. Maybe I don't get to decide what's right or wrong anymore.

As he walks, his foot brushes against one of the scattered photographs from the mess earlier. He bends down and picks it up with surprising gentleness. It's an old war photo of Grandma Gerta—the one where her wild, intense eyes stare straight ahead, full of some fierce, private emotion. Saul stares at it, unmoving. Time stretches thin, pulling me back to that night in the cemetery—tripping over uneven ground, everything narrowing into a single, frozen moment. I hadn't needed to read the name on the gravestone. I had already known who was buried beneath it.

Saul lifts the photograph closer, his fingers moving with slow care, as if he's holding something sacred. Then, after a moment, he turns to me.

Without saying a word, he reaches out, his large hands cradling my face. His touch is gentle, careful—like I'm something fragile. He strokes my cheeks, his fingers gliding over my lips with the lightest pressure. His thumb lingers at my lower lip before his whole hand covers my mouth.

For the first time, he looks at peace. Almost… happy.

My eyes flick toward the mirror in the corner. The reflection staring back at me is not my own.

It's her.

Grandma Gerta's fierce face, filled with strength and beauty, gazes back at me. And in that moment, I can't tell where she ends and I begin.

Now I am in bed. My eyes are closed, my lips slightly parted. The air is thick with the scent of hot earth. Ashes swirl in the darkness, brushing against my skin like whispered secrets. Saul leans over me, his breath warm and deep. He pulls me toward him, and then his lips are on mine, firm, unrelenting.

The kiss consumes me.

Our mouths press together, tangled in a feverish need, as though something inside us is burning. My lips tingle, almost as if they're melting under his touch. The heat spreads, searing, as if the kiss itself is made of fire. My skin feels like it's bubbling, soft and fragile.

I know that even when the kiss ends—if it ever ends—we'll still be connected. There will be something between us, thin and stretched tight, impossible to break.

But right now, none of that matters.

Let this kiss last forever, I think. Let it pull me under completely. Let me disappear into it.

Then—

A pounding knock shatters the silence.

My eyes snap open. The world slams back into focus, crushing me beneath its weight.

Someone is at the door, knocking hard. Again and again.

The sound is relentless, sharp, and urgent.

Whoever it is, they need to get in.

Damn it.

"Telma, open the door."

Simon's voice is firm, slicing through the silence. My heart jumps as I leap out of bed and rush to the mirror. My reflection stares back—flushed lips, dark circles under my eyes, and a tense expression I can't shake. It's nothing Simon hasn't seen before, I tell myself. But still, he's the last person I want to face right now. Well, second to last.

I reach the door but hesitate. Not the time for grudges, I remind myself, even though just hearing his voice makes my stomach twist.

"What do you want?" I ask, keeping my voice calm, maybe even a little distant. Just enough to remind him of what he did with Nili— something I haven't forgotten.

"Why didn't you answer my calls yesterday?" His tone is sharp. I can tell he's suspicious.

"I was busy," I say with a shrug.

"With what?" His eyes scan the room, searching for something— anything—that might explain what's really going on. I lean against the doorframe, trying to look casual, but he pushes past me and steps inside. So much for staying in control.

"Is everything okay?" His eyes narrow as he studies me.

Something in his expression makes me extra careful with my words. "Yeah, I'm fine," I say, steady and even.

But he doesn't believe me. I force a small smile, pretending everything is normal, but it feels forced, unnatural. The effort is exhausting. Even the room feels different, like something's slightly off. Is it just me, or has that mold stain on the wall gotten smaller?

A wave of panic crashes over me. What if Saul suddenly walks out of the attic? The thought is unbearable. Simon seeing Saul—or worse, Saul seeing Simon—is a disaster waiting to happen. But Saul won't come out, right? I haven't told him to. That should be enough. Shouldn't it? I barely know what he's capable of.

Simon needs to leave. Fast.

"What do you want?" I ask again, but this time my voice is tight, high-pitched. Too obvious.

Simon watches me carefully. "Something's up," he says, suspicion dripping from every word. "I don't know what, but… you look different."

Different.

The word lands like a crack in the surface of my mind, shifting the way I see him. For the first time, he seems smaller, paler—his skin dull, like the ghostly white mushrooms that grow in dark places. And his lips… dry, lifeless. Were these the lips that once made my whole body burn? The same lips that used to pull me in so easily?

I stare at them, and they part.

"Telma," he says. "About Seder night—"

Any other day, I might have apologized. I might have played along, told him Nili's dress was an accident, reassured him that he could be with whoever he wanted.

But not today.

"What about Seder night?" I interrupt before he can launch into whatever excuse he's been rehearsing. His face shifts, thrown off. For a second, he just stares at me, confused—like he doesn't understand why I'm not following the usual script.

"I just wanted to make sure you were okay," he says at last, voice uncertain. "I didn't want to leave things like this before I go abroad."

My stomach tightens. "Where are you going?" I ask, keeping my tone light.

"Poland. Today. The March of the Living starts right after Passover this year."

Of course. How could I forget? Another trip to wander through cemeteries, sifting through dirt, chasing the ghosts of our past. Seems like that's the real family tradition.

"Your dad's been after me about some documents from Warsaw," Simon adds. "Something about an old building your family owned. He wants me to track it down while I'm there."

Then—I hear something. A faint sound from the attic.

My head tilts slightly, listening, my body tense. Simon notices immediately. His frown deepens, his suspicion growing.

"Are you sure everything's okay?" His voice is sharper now, pressing me for answers.

I take a breath. And then, before I can stop myself, the words slip out.

"Tell me, Simon," I say, my voice raw. "Do you love her?"

Golem or no golem, I have to ask. Because at the end of the day, Simon was here first. And we're talking about Nili—my cousin, my coworker, my lifelong rival. The girl who always seems to be one step ahead of me.

He hesitates. Then another noise comes from the attic.

"Yes," he finally says. "I think I do."

The words cut straight through me.

Two eyes, two lips, one heart, one emptiness.

Which one is more beautiful? He answers without hesitation.

And suddenly, I find myself capable of giving a command—at least in my mind. Kill! I scream silently. Tear him apart!

But Saul is in the attic. And I am still standing here, face to face with Simon.

He watches me closely, his expression shifting between relief and suspicion. Later, when he's on his flight to Warsaw, he'll probably think, She handled that pretty well. He might even tell Nili.

But what he won't see—what no one will see—is the look on my face once I close the door behind him.

Now is the time for tears.

I've always believed that forcing a smile is the quickest way to make yourself cry. The body reacts, like it has to balance out fake happiness with real sadness. And crying? Crying is easier. Tears are natural. Smiling through pain takes effort.

I sink onto the living room carpet. I could say I soak it with my tears, but the truth is, there are none. My tears don't fall—they cut. They stay locked inside, sharp and jagged, like tiny shards of glass pressing behind my eyes. They scrape and burn, but they never spill over.

I cry for Simon. For Nili. For the years I lost. For Grandma Gerta. For myself. Even for Saul.

How could I have been so blind? I always thought I was weak, but smart enough to make up for it. Smart enough to be dangerous one day. But now I see myself clearly.

I was wrong.

I am small. Unimportant. Forgettable. Unloved.

The pain is unbearable. I collapse onto my hands and knees, my forehead pressed into the carpet. The position is familiar—too familiar. As familiar as the empty space inside me where all my tears should be.

But this time, someone hears me.

He lifts me gently, holding me close.

Saul.

I feel his warmth, steady and strong. His wound has healed—his skin is smooth, unmarked. My hands move over him, searching, but he stops them, holding them in his own. His hands burn like fire.

He tilts my face up toward his.

And then I see it. The sadness in his eyes.

It's for me.

All of it.

A tear finally falls, sliding down my cheek. I want to bury my face in his chest, to lose myself in his warmth, but I hesitate. What happens if my tears touch his burning skin?

Saul moves slowly, brushing them away with his fingers. Mud smears across my skin, and thin wisps of steam rise where his touch lingers. Pain flickers in his eyes, but he is so gentle, so careful, that I can't stop the tears from coming.

Something stirs inside me, small and delicate. It flutters, like a tiny heartbeat. Could this be happiness? I don't know. I have nothing to compare it to.

I look up at him.

My lips tingle, aching for what comes next. The kiss.

The one I've imagined. The one that finally feels real.

I lean in, my whole body drawn to him, and press my lips toward his.

But just before I reach him, Saul turns his head away.

The shock hits me like ice water.

The rejection slams into me, but even worse than the rejection itself is the fact that I never expected it.

This wasn't supposed to happen.

It feels wrong—like a mistake, an error in how things were meant to go. I had been so certain. That certainty was what gave me the courage to reach for him in the first place. And yet, here I am.

Rejected.

In any other situation, I'd be embarrassed. I'd worry about bad breath or food in my teeth.

But not now. Not with him.

Because even as he turns away, he doesn't let go of me. He still holds me close. His body burns against mine, his eyes full of something I can't quite name.

I can feel his desire—it mirrors my own, maybe even greater. But that only makes the rejection more confusing, more painful.

And yet, I know—without a doubt—the kiss already happened.

I felt it. Everywhere.

It filled the air, it filled me.

So why does it feel like it disappeared? Like it was never real?

Where did it go?

And why—why—did he pull away?

The questions won't stop. They press in on me, suffocating. But none of them change the way I feel about him. None of them erase the bond between us, the connection that wraps around me, stronger than anything I've ever known.

And then, just as the thought takes hold, another one crashes through.

A cold, undeniable truth.

He is not a living thing, Telma.

Chapter 15

Everything that happens to us leaves a mark—inside and out.

What we call "facial features" are really just muscles and tendons waiting beneath the skin, shifting and shaping with every experience. Every feeling, every moment, leaves its trace, telling the world our story whether we want it to or not. Our faces reveal us, exposing things we might prefer to keep hidden. Maybe that's why they wear out so quickly. It's not just aging, like beauty magazines claim—it's the weight of emotions, the constant pull of what we've been through.

It's not gravity that makes a face change. It's life. Eyes that have seen too much grow heavy. A nose that has smelled fear sharpens, as if stretching away from danger. Ears sag, burdened by words they were never meant to hear. Anger clenches a jaw, twisting it into something almost wild. Every line, every shadow, is a road map of everything we've survived.

One day, people might cover their faces the way they cover their bodies. For now, we settle for masks.

And mine? Mine is the ugliest of all.

I stare at myself in the bathroom mirror, studying every curve, every line. My lips, untouched by any kiss, press together tightly, hardened by disappointment. I run my fingers across my skin, feeling the slight slickness of morning oil. Most days, my face is so greasy when I wake up that it feels like a frying pan. But today, it looks calm—giving away nothing. Still, I keep looking, waiting for it to betray me.

As I brush my teeth, Saul appears in the doorway, leaning against the frame. His blurred shape lingers in the mirror, his outline soft behind my sharper reflection. I wipe the steam from the glass, but even then, he stays hazy, like he belongs to another world.

The toothpaste in my mouth turns thick and foamy, and I spit it out, my head tilting back up to find him still watching me.

I should be used to the way he looks at me by now, the way his gaze lingers, slow and deliberate. But this time, it feels different—deeper, more invasive. His eyes don't just glance over me; they seem to reach inside, exploring parts of me I've never shared with anyone. It's like he's speaking to my insides—my kidneys, my lungs, my ovaries. No matter how many layers I wear, I feel completely exposed in front of him.

And the thought of him seeing me without those layers? It makes my stomach tighten. When will that happen? whispers a voice in my head. You dirty girl.

A naked body can't hide anything. Every scar, every flaw, every secret is out in the open. There's no pretending. No mask.

Saul keeps his gaze on my face, which is now dripping with white foam. I wonder what he's holding inside those closed lips. That tiny slip of paper—small, powerful, unreachable. What happens when I need it back? It's not yours, something inside me reminds me.

I lean closer to the mirror to put in my contact lenses. The thin, glassy discs sting as they settle into place, and the bathroom sharpens around me. My eyes land on a forgotten pair of pantyhose behind the door, already growing mold. On the mirror, a faint circle of steam lingers where my breath touched the glass. Saul stares at it.

Later, I'll catch him in the same spot, breathing against the mirror again and again, as if testing something. His reflection stays clear, unchanged. No fog. No warmth. Not even the faintest sign of breath. He exhales forcefully, trying to make something appear, willing himself to leave a trace of heat in this world.

In the kitchen, I set the table for one, just like I did in my loneliest days. Slices of pink peaches, soft cheese, brown rolls, a perfectly poached egg. I drink cold water straight from the grimy faucet, the icy chill stabbing my teeth. I don't dare spill anything near Saul.

He sits across from me, motionless, silent, eating nothing.

What keeps him going? What fuels this man made of earth? Are the letters under his tongue enough to sustain him, the way certain words steal the breath from my lungs? MY. SAUL. The thought is oddly comforting, though I'd never say it out loud. The idea of becoming one of those lovesick fools, asking if he sees a future with me, if he'll always be mine—it makes me shiver.

Saul watches me. His lips curl slightly, almost like a smirk, as if he can hear my thoughts.

His presence across the table is overwhelming. His form is too solid, too real. The weight of it presses against me, stirring something deep in my stomach—a discomfort so thick it feels like a snail crawling down my thigh, leaving behind a sticky, shameful trail.

I push back from the table, standing abruptly. This has to stop.

I rush to my grandmother's old closet. My grandfather was tall, strong—like Saul. His old suits still hang alongside the summer dresses.

Without thinking, I grab a few shirts and throw them at Saul. Harder than necessary.

I wonder what Grandma Gerta would think if she saw this—if she knew what I was doing with her late husband's clothes.

The thought makes my skin crawl. But I can't stop thinking about it.

I try to picture Grandpa Andrei, but his face is as blurry in my mind as Saul's was in the mirror earlier. All I can remember is a kind smile—one that reminds me of Bella's mischievous grin. But now, I wonder if that smile wasn't pure kindness. Maybe it was the quiet acceptance of someone who lived without love.

Grandma Gerta didn't love him enough. She never looked at him with warmth, never rested her hand on his arm, never laughed with him the way she did in that old wartime photograph. Maybe she only felt alive in moments of danger, in the rush of survival. Maybe a steady, safe love like Andrei's was too dull for her.

And the worst thought of all—am I just like her? Do I need chaos, destruction, and risk to actually feel something?

My hands clench into fists. The dry skin scrapes against itself, rough and peeling. I glance down and notice tiny cracks forming on my knuckles, like my body is reflecting the emptiness inside me.

I lift my eyes back to Saul. He hasn't moved. One of my grandfather's shirts rests on his knees, draped like a napkin at a fancy dinner.

"You need to get dressed," I say. But even as I say it, another thought creeps in. Why? Who else is going to see him but me?

Why cover up something so perfect?

His body is everything I am not. His dark, earthy skin looks like it was shaped straight from the soil of the cemetery, while mine is pale, almost colorless. My round face and weak chin are nothing compared to his sharp, sculpted jawline. The bump on my nose has no match on his perfectly straight profile. His lips are full, rich in color, while mine are thin, like a cruel joke.

And then there's the way he carries himself—tall, steady, unshaken. His strong shoulders hold him upright while I shrink under the weight of my own thoughts. Next to him, the top of my head barely reaches his neck.

It feels right, though.

My eyes drift downward, stopping just before I let myself go too far. Beneath those sculpted muscles, there is more beauty. More strength.

But I can't look.

I tell myself it's because of modesty, because of the way I was raised. But the truth is, I feel a heat pooling deep inside me, a strange shame pressing against my skin.

Being naked must have a reason, I think. It can't just exist without meaning.

"Get dressed," I say again, sharper this time.

Saul picks up the shirt, turning it over in his hands as if searching for something hidden. Then, slowly, he lifts it to his face and sniffs it. He stands still for a moment, as if thinking—then, without warning, he rips it apart.

One strip at a time.

The sound of tearing fabric fills the room, each rip slow and deliberate. His movements are steady, controlled. It doesn't feel like an act of rebellion. It feels… ritualistic.

I stare at him, frozen. Should I be angry? Amused?

A ridiculous thought crosses my mind—maybe he has his own sense of style. Maybe my golem is a fashion critic.

I should laugh at the absurdity of it.

But instead, a strange excitement rises in me.

He didn't listen to me. And that gives me the perfect reason to buy him a shirt myself.

For the first time in my life, I will walk into a men's clothing store and choose something for someone who belongs to me.

I picture it so clearly—walking into the store, standing tall, telling the saleswoman, "I need a shirt for a broad-shouldered man." I imagine the flicker of envy in her eyes as she wonders about the man I'm shopping for.

This simple act—so normal, so routine—will make Saul real in a way that nothing else has.

The thought fills me with purpose.

The shop will be bright, filled with busy saleswomen clicking their heels against the polished floor. They will flutter around, calling to each other in sharp voices, their arms draped with clothes.

I know exactly the kind of woman they are. I have feared them my whole life.

They move in packs, circling thin, elegant customers, their voices dripping with praise—"It's perfect!" Their confidence is unshakable, their opinions absolute.

To them, I have always been nothing. Either invisible or embarrassingly obvious.

They have a way of looking at you, slicing through you with a single glance—sizing up your hips, your outfit, your worth. Their dismissive looks have pushed me out of stores so many times, but not before I grabbed something—anything—just to avoid the shame of walking out empty-handed.

I've left stores clutching skirts that didn't fit, shirts that clung in all the wrong places, clothes that would sit in the back of my closet, untouched. I never wanted their approval, but I always felt their judgment.

I remember the worst of it—the way they smirked as I bought a hideous brocade skirt, their contempt following me out the door.

But this time, I won't be shopping for myself.

This time, I will belong in that store. Because this time, I am buying something for him.

But today is different. Not this time.

My heels tap confidently—click-clack, click-clack—as I walk across the store, feeling like I belong. One of the saleswomen notices me from a distance, her sharp eyes scanning me, sizing me up as she strides over, confident like a hunter moving in on its prey.

"Excuse me," I say, lifting my chin just a little. "I'm looking for a men's shirt." My voice is steady, my expression calm. It works—her gaze softens, losing its edge.

"He's tall, broad-shouldered, dark-skinned," I continue, letting each word land with weight. I watch as her posture changes, the authority fading from her stance. By the time I finish speaking, she no longer looks like an intimidating saleswoman—just another person, one who probably curls up alone at night, just like the rest of us.

"I'll bring some shirts right away," she says, her tone almost respectful now. "Does he—or you—have a color preference?"

"There's only one choice," I say with a small smile. "Navy blue."

She hurries off and returns with a few options, but none of them feel right. "Would you like me to bring more?" she asks, eager to please. I nod, watching her rush back and forth until finally, she brings the perfect one. Large, rich, a deep blue that matches exactly what I had in mind. Satisfaction settles over me.

For the first time, I feel like someone. Like a woman choosing clothes for her man.

Confidence surges through me. "Actually," I say, as if the thought just came to me, "I'd like to try something on for myself." Not this time, little shopgirl—no more awful skirts that don't fit.

I leave the store triumphant, my arms full of shopping bags. I take the stairs two at a time, each step feeling like a small victory—over loneliness, over doubt, over the parts of myself I've spent years trying to hide. I can't wait to see him wear it, to see how my choice fits him.

Outside a nearby apartment, a small boy sits on the doorstep, his head resting in his hands, staring at the ground. It's one of Haya's kids, usually nosy and full of questions. But today, he doesn't look at me. His whole posture seems weighed down by something heavy.

"Congratulations," I say gently, but he doesn't lift his head.

"What did your mom have?" I ask, my voice soft, playful. I know it's the wrong approach—kids are smarter than we give them credit for, and pretending doesn't fool them. But I can't help myself. "A boy or a girl?"

"Boys," he mutters, eyes fixed on a tiny gecko trapped in the corner.

"Twins?" I exclaim, forcing some enthusiasm. "That's amazing!"

I lean in, meaning to give him a quick hug, but he pulls away like I might burn him.

"What are their names?" I ask, then immediately regret it. "Oh, never mind—you'll tell us at the bris, right?"

"No," he mumbles, barely above a whisper. "There won't be a bris."

I try to guess. "Oh, because they're too small?"

"No!" His voice cracks, and something in him seems to break. "Because they're attached!"

Then he bolts, shouting over his shoulder, "Ugly freaks!"

The shopping bags slip from my hands.

When I walk into the apartment, Saul is standing there, buttoning up the shirt I bought for him.

It fits perfectly.

The deep blue fabric clings to his body, showing every sharp angle, every strong line. The color matches the veins under his skin, and I can't stop staring. He looks whole. Flawless. Perfect.

Unlike—

I push the thought away.

"Wait," I say, stepping toward him. "Let me do it."

I finish buttoning the shirt, smoothing the fabric into place, tucking it into his dark trousers. The act feels strangely tender—like dressing a child. But at the same time, there's something else, something electric that makes every nerve in my body feel too aware, too alive.

That feeling returns—that awful, sticky sensation, like a slow-moving snail dragging itself down my thigh, leaving behind something slick and humiliating. My body is leaking want, and I press my legs together, trying to make it stop.

Saul watches me the whole time.

A slow, knowing smirk plays on his lips.

It's mocking. Teasing. Like he's daring me to say it out loud. Go ahead. Ask me. Tell me what you want.

But he knows I won't. He knows I can't.

Because asking would mean exposing everything—admitting the need, the hunger, the shame of wanting him this much.

I can't do it.

Because if I ask, there's a chance he'll say no. And if he does, that would prove what I've feared all along—that I am unworthy. That I am unlovable.

Saul seems to understand this. He waits, his silence thick with power.

And I hate him for it.

Bastard.

The knock on the door makes me jump.

It's loud, firm, impatient. Let me in. Let me in.

I already know who it is.

Since the day I moved in, this door has been nothing but a portal for unwanted guests—people who bring nothing but stress, criticism, and unwanted advice.

My stomach twists. But I force it down. Calm down, Telma. Act normal.

I open the door, trying to keep my face neutral.

But inside, I'm already seething.

They sweep inside—my parents.

Or, as I call them in my head: Gila and Reuven. The original architects of my self-doubt. My natural-born enemies.

My father sniffs the air, already looking for something to disapprove of. My mother clutches a plastic shopping bag, something bulky and woolen inside.

I can already tell what it is.

A hideous, oversized sweatsuit.

I swallow back the urge to snap, I sleep naked, Mother. What exactly do you think I need that for?

"What a surprise," I say, quickly grabbing newspapers and scattered photos from the couch. With a nudge of my foot, I slide a few candy wrappers under the armchair, suddenly hyper-aware of the mess everywhere. The clutter, the dust—how did I not notice it before?

"Why didn't you let me know you were coming?" I add, keeping my voice light, aiming for the polite surprise of a host caught off guard.

Reuven narrows his eyes. He doesn't buy it. He moves through the room like some oversized rodent, pausing to inspect a needlepoint tapestry I turned to face the wall.

"But Telma," my mother says, her voice carrying just the right amount of exasperation to irritate me, "I told you we were coming a few days after Seder to collect Grandma's holy books for the synagogue donation. I even mentioned it at the table."

Of course, I don't remember this at all. The Seder was a blur— too much noise, too much wine. When exactly was she supposed to have said this? While Moses glared at me from the Haggadah illustrations? While I was drinking Elijah's wine? I picture that accusing face now, sneering, Daughter of Egypt! Little Pharaoh!

Maybe they made the whole thing up, knowing I'd been too out of it to object.

They settle in like they own the place, reclaiming lost territory. My father leans back, slurping his lukewarm tea, each noisy sip clawing at my nerves. I clench my fists and think, Choke on it, Reuven. Just choke.

My mother hovers awkwardly, unsure where to place the bag holding that awful sweatsuit. Her eyes sweep across the room, taking in every inch of dust, every faded photograph, every crooked stack of books. I can feel her judgment without her saying a word. She catalogues every failure, every sign of neglect. Then, finally, she looks at me. I feel that gaze like a weight pressing down on my chest.

And just like that, they pull me into their world.

It's not what they say. It's not even what they do. It's them. Their presence, their endless cycle of disappointment and small, tired dreams.

My father, always talking about the Warsaw house we'll never see again. My mother, always listing her aches and pains. And me—their daughter—slowly becoming them, trapped in the same pattern, tethered to their life by something invisible but unbreakable.

I see it so clearly: the sighing, the slurping, the endless complaints. And worst of all, the creeping realization that I'm becoming like them.

The thought makes my stomach turn.

Tears push at the edges of my eyes, frustration rising in my throat. But something stops them, holds them back. The usual flood of emotions doesn't come. Instead, there's something else—something grounding me, keeping me steady.

Wait. There's something more important right now.

And there is.

The attic feels warmer than usual, like it's holding its breath. Saul stands there, still as a statue, his dark blue shirt making him look almost festive.

But he's calm. Completely calm.

And that calm reaches me, cooling the fire inside, yet at the same time, making something else stir. Something sharp and alive.

"My parents are downstairs," I whisper, as if saying it too loudly might summon them.

His expression shifts—just slightly. A flicker of something in his dark eyes, something almost amused.

That tiny smirk infuriates me.

As if he's enjoying this. As if watching me squirm is entertainment.

"Please, try not to make any noise," I say, stepping closer.

The space between us thickens.

I can feel my body waking up under his gaze, like every inch of skin has suddenly become aware of itself. The air crackles between us, full of heat and something dangerous, something unspoken.

It's not just want. It's need.

And for once, it doesn't make me feel weak. It makes me feel alive.

Downstairs, my parents sit like ghosts, sipping their weak tea, clinging to their dull, gray existence. Their world is stale, filled with regrets and empty routines.

And I want Saul to pull me away from it.

To burn me up.

To take me into something real.

But I can't say it.

Ask him. Tell him. Command him. Beg him.

No.

The words lodge in my throat, heavy and stuck. Why do things always have to be said out loud? Why do words always betray me?

My whole life has been a series of almosts. Almost saying the right thing. Almost choosing the right path. Always walking next to happiness, but never stepping into it.

And now, I stand beside him, close enough to feel the heat of his skin, and I still can't say the words.

He watches me with maddening patience, as if to say, Sorry, but I can't read minds, Madame.

Downstairs, silence lingers in the air, thick with unspoken words.

I feel it before I even enter the room.

My parents glance at me with that mix of concern and irritation they've perfected over the years. I don't react. Instead, I open a packet of stale crackers, breaking them in my hands. They taste like dust and soap, but I chew them anyway, letting the crunch fill the emptiness.

The boxes slowly fill with books—Grandma's old religious texts, packed up for donation.

But I don't care. The only book that matters is hidden far beyond their reach.

My father rifles through the shelves, his nosy energy as strong as ever. My mother stands beside him, blinking rapidly, her face caught between disapproval and exhaustion. She looks like an old owl, her head twitching as she scans the spines of the books.

Behind her, the needlepoint fawn on the wall smiles its eternal, empty smile.

"So, Simon's off to Poland, huh?" my father says suddenly, holding up a worn book like some grand discovery. His tone is sharp, pointed, filled with something smug.

The meaning is clear.

So, you couldn't keep him, could you?

窗体顶端

窗体底端

I stay silent, my eyes locked on the book in his hands. I shouldn't have left it there. What other mistakes have I made?

"I gave him a small job," Father says, clearly enjoying this topic.

"There's a man in Warsaw who says he has documents proving the house belonged to us. A respectable Jewish family. None of this hero nonsense." He shoots a sharp look at Mother.

And just like that, the argument begins. The same one they've had for years. They know their lines by heart, their voices rising and falling in a familiar rhythm.

Mother snaps back, her tone cold. "You only say that because your family's house is still full of Poles! You can't give my mother credit for getting hers back."

I don't need to listen to know what comes next. Their fights are as predictable as the tide. Accusations thrown back and forth, like a routine they refuse to break.

"Oh sure, big-time rebels!" Father scoffs, clearing his throat like he's about to land the final blow.

Mother waves him off, her expression tight. They're stuck in this endless cycle, locked in a battle neither of them will ever win. Maybe they don't even want to. Maybe this fight is all they have left holding them together.

Then—THUD. A sudden, loud noise from the attic.

They freeze, both heads snapping toward the ceiling.

"What was that?" Father's voice is sharp with suspicion.

Panic rises in my throat, and I blurt out, "Oh, that? Just... uh... the Passover dishes. Nili's stuff. I haven't sorted them yet, and everything's stacked too high. Super unstable. Last night two big pots fell, scared me half to death, blah blah blah..."

I stop too late. Their eyes narrow at the same time. Suspicion replaces curiosity. Why didn't I just brush it off? Why didn't I just say,

None of your business, you nosy jerks?

I race upstairs, skipping steps, my heart pounding. I burst into the attic, and there's Saul, leaning against the wall like he belongs here. Like this is his home.

"What are you doing?" I hiss, my voice sharp and panicked. "Already planning to meet the family?" My sarcasm lingers in the air between us. Can a golem even understand irony? I don't care to find out.

My voice turns serious, cutting through my panic. "You will not move until they leave." The words leave my mouth like a blade, sharp and absolute.

Before my eyes, Saul changes. His strong, vibrant body seems to deflate. His muscles go slack, his posture limp like a puppet with cut strings. But his eyes—still burning, still full of life—lock onto me in silent protest. He has to obey. But I can feel his resistance in that stare.

This is it—my first real command. So why does it feel so wrong? Why is the first thing I do take away the very life I want from him? The thought twists inside me. My face burns with shame. I can't look at him anymore. I pull away, even though I'm standing right in front of him.

"I'll be right down!" I call over my shoulder, my voice shaky. I flee, but something inside me cracks open, spilling through me like fire. I press my legs together, trying to hold it in.

Downstairs, Gila and Reuven stand by the door. Their job is done. Boxes packed, shelves emptied, their duty as parents performed with cold precision. Their concern is just an act, lingering in the air like cheap perfume.

I walk them to the door, desperate for them to leave so I can run back to the attic. Back to Saul. Back to whatever is happening inside me.

Father pauses, his small eyes narrowing as he stares at me. He smells the change in me, the secrets I carry.

Without warning, his hand shoots out, gripping my arm tightly.

"I see," he whispers, his face too close. "Don't think for a second that I don't see."

Our eyes lock. His cold blue against my gray. Father against daughter. Years of anger, blame, and something deeper—something neither of us will say out loud—pass between us.

I yank my arm free like his touch burns me. "Don't you dare touch me, you piece of shit," I spit, my voice shaking with fury. "You—"

Before I can finish, his hand swings up and smacks across my face.

The impact is like a gunshot. My head snaps back, slamming into the fuse box. Stars burst behind my eyes. My skin burns. My ears ring.

I stand there, stunned.

I have been slapped.

This man, this father of nothing, just hit me.

"Reuven!" Mother gasps, shocked, but she doesn't move.

A deep, burning rage rises inside me, wild and unstoppable. I see flashes in my mind—Father lying crumpled under the fuse box, his neck bent at a terrible angle, his empty eyes staring at nothing. Blood. Pain. Death. Mother sobbing over his body. Me standing at his grave, feeling nothing. My fists tighten, and suddenly, I understand—I could do it. My hands, so small just moments ago, could destroy him.

I take a step forward, shaking with fury. He steps back, his face going pale, then turns and runs down the stairs. Mother follows, slower, her eyes filled with confusion and fear. Neither of them looks back. That's for the best. They wouldn't recognize me now—their little girl with a red cheek and wild eyes.

The insult stings as I rush up the stairs again, my feet moving faster than my thoughts. My face throbs where he struck me, my teeth clenched so hard I can feel the pain in my gums. My whole body feels like it's being torn apart, something inside me scratching to get out. My hands ache, my knuckles white.

Saul is waiting, his steady brown eyes watching me. He reaches out and presses his warm palm against my burning cheek. The touch is gentle, grounding me, pulling me back from the edge. I lean into him, the fire inside me cooling into something softer. His touch soothes me, but it can't take away what just happened.

I take his hand, leading him downstairs, moving forward with a certainty I don't fully understand. We head toward Grandma Gerta's room, a place heavy with fate, as if this moment was always meant to happen—long before I ever shaped him from the earth.

Something inside me has answered a call.

That truth settles over me, clear and sharp, separate from my tangled desires. I let him wrap me in his arms. I let him claim me. I am ready for this war, this battle that will define me. Everything that broke me led me here. And everything that prepared me has destroyed the rest.

Maybe love has nothing to do with it at all.

Around the bed, small figures appear, little versions of Telma, holding hands. Their laughter is light but eerie. They sway in a circle, singing in soft, haunting voices:

From earth and blood you knead the dough
Watch until it rises so
Bake it and it turns to man
Man then bakes you back again.

Oh yes, he will bake me back again. He will shape me, press his hands into my skin, and shove me into an oven until I come out changed—just like him.

We are so close now that his stillness presses against me like a wall. I breathe out, but there's no breath coming back from him. No movement. Then, a realization strikes me with terrifying clarity—he won't do anything until I tell him to. My hunger, my trembling, my burning desire—it all means nothing to him.

I brush my fingers against his chest, but he doesn't react. My body is aching, desperate, but he stands there, waiting. You pathetic, powerless woman.

The room is stifling, thick with heat that clings to my skin, making me sweat. Drops of moisture slide down my temples, down my neck, slipping between my breasts, pooling between my thighs. The heat grows, pulsing through me like a wave, but even this fire isn't enough to force the words out of my mouth.

I can't ask.

To say it out loud would be to admit the truth—to expose my weakness, my need. The words I refuse to say trap my shame inside me. This is my sin, raw and unforgiving.

And this man, standing before me, is the proof of that sin. He watches me with knowing eyes, taunting me. Go on, his gaze seems to say. Ask for it. Show me who you really are, doll.

The shame burns deep. I swallow hard, my throat dry.

"Please," I whisper, my voice shaking.

Still, he does not move.

The heat from his body seems alive, wrapping around me, suffocating and electrifying at the same time. My fingertips graze his chest again, and this time, the touch feels like fire licking my skin. My whole body throbs, my need so sharp it feels like it might tear me apart.

"Please," I try again, voice barely above a breath.

"Please, kiss me..."

Slowly, he lowers his head. His lips hover near mine, unbearably close. I can see the slight curve of his mouth. And in that moment, I know—he is smiling. And that smile is anything but kind.

"On my lips," I whisper, my voice breaking. My legs tremble beneath me.

His lips brush the corner of my mouth, my chin, the crease below my nose—light, indifferent kisses that set my skin on fire. They are not the kisses I begged for, but they still burn me to my core. And with each teasing touch, my last shred of resistance shatters.

He has won.

"Do it to me," I plead, unable to name what I want. The words themselves are humiliating, an admission of defeat. "Do it." My voice is unsteady, thick with fear and shame. "Do it hard, do it with force."

He grips my shoulders and lifts me off the ground with ease, his expression unreadable. He moves mechanically, like a puppet. Our eyes meet, and for a moment, he hesitates, as if considering what my words really mean.

"Please, have mercy," I whisper, my voice raw. "Don't make me keep asking... I won't say anything more..."

And just like that, he gives in.

He surrenders to the force we all pretend we can control. That thing inside us we try to separate from, but never truly can. Something inside him breaks, and suddenly, he is alive.

His hands grip me hard, molding me, pressing me into something new. He crushes me against him, and I feel it—fire, earth, power. And I knew, even before I shaped him from the dirt, that this was inevitable.

Somewhere far away, I hear flames crackling. The sound of something breaking inside me.

This is the end.

This is the beginning.

When it's over, the sheets are covered in dirt. Clumps of soil fall from my body as I move. I still feel the sting of the slap from earlier, the echo of it lingering on my skin.

I deserve it.

I am no longer human. I am a mannequin now, too—a hollow figure, trapped in a body reshaped by fire and earth, remade in his image.

Chapter 17

Love is reflection of the self.

Telma stares into Saul's deep, earth-colored eyes and sees herself reflected back. What does she find there? Admiration, yes. Curiosity, definitely. And hidden between those emotions, something that almost looks like joy.

She watches how he reacts to her—the way he lingers on her face, the way his body responds to her touch, the way his eyes follow her every move. In that moment, something clicks inside her. For the first time in her life, Telma loves Telma.

I lie on Grandma Gerta's big bed, Saul's dark head resting against my arm. A strange sense of calm washes over me, softening the sharp, restless parts of me. My fingers trace gentle lines over his face, pausing on each feature I once shaped with my own hands. He is so still, so peaceful, and I let myself believe that means he is content. But deep down, I wonder—could it be something else?

What is he thinking about as he lies beside me? How does his golem-mind understand what we do here, in this bed, in this room? When I look into his dark eyes and see my reflection, do I see the real me? Or just what I want to believe?

I almost ask him. Almost. The words sit on my tongue: What are you thinking? But I can't bring myself to say them.

I have never told him to love me. Even I know love isn't something you can force. But that doesn't stop me from wondering—what is love? Could a being made of earth and willpower even feel it? He is gentle when he touches me, careful, almost reverent. Is that real? Or is he simply acting as he was created to?

The thought strikes me like a slap. If his kindness is just instinct, if it's built into him instead of freely given, then I will rip the paper from his mouth and watch him crumble back into the dirt he came from. If he isn't choosing this, then it isn't real. And if it isn't real, then I have been fooling myself.

But isn't this what you wanted, Telma?

No. Not anymore.

Now, Telma wants something else.

She wonders if love can grow on its own, without commands or control. She imagines tiny flowers sprouting from his dark body, vines curling around his wrists, delicate petals blooming on his head. If only love worked that way—obvious, visible, undeniable. Humans don't have that luxury. They fill the air with sweet words, empty promises, clever lies. But Saul… Saul can't lie. Or can he?

I search his eyes for answers. Do they soften when he looks at me? Do they lighten, just a little, as if something deeper is rising to the surface? Or am I just seeing what I want to see?

But none of that matters right now. Because at this moment, I am happy.

The bed beneath us grows dirtier every day, but I don't care.

The missing stack of history exams spills from my teacher's bag as I adjust my hair in the mirror. I crouch to pick them up, unwilling to let those terrible wartime stories seep into this space, into this part of my life. My fingers slide through my dark hair—it feels fuller, healthier, more alive than ever before.

I glance at Saul, sitting quietly on the bed, waiting.

"How do I look?" My voice is lower, huskier now, roughened by the changes in me. This new voice forces me to choose my words carefully, giving everything I say an unintentional sharpness.

As always, Saul listens. His dark eyes lock onto mine, steady, unblinking. His gaze makes me blush—an unfamiliar feeling. He doesn't look at me like a creation looking at its maker. No, he looks at me like a man looking at a woman.

And how perfect it is.

There is no one else for him to compare me to, no impossible standards I must meet. To him, I am it. I am beauty itself, without flaw, without competition. My body, every soft or imperfect part, is enough. This is how things should be. Simple. Right.

I step toward him, hesitating only for a moment before pressing my hand to the lighter patch of skin on his chest. I sit beside him, and he buries his head in my chest, wrapping his arms around me. I close my eyes, letting myself melt into the moment, letting myself believe that this feeling will last forever.

"Saul," I murmur, "I'll be late for school."

Then I see it.

In the corner of the room, a tiny gecko twists in the shadows, its nearly see-through tails flickering in and out of the light. Saul tenses in my arms, and suddenly, the air in the room feels different. Something unspoken lingers between us.

Disgust twists in my stomach. My skin turns pale as I stare at the writhing little creature, its two tails twitching in a way that makes my whole body shudder. But Saul doesn't move. He just stands there, frozen, his deep brown eyes locked on the gecko with an intensity that unsettles me.

"Kill it!" I scream, my voice raw and cracking.

He hesitates.

Rage surges through me, and I shriek, my throat burning from the force of it. "Kill that thing!"

Slowly, as if reluctant, Saul steps toward the corner. He reaches down and grabs the gecko by one of its flailing tails. The creature thrashes in his grip as he closes his fingers around it. His movements are oddly gentle, but his eyes hold something deeper—something I can't quite understand. His hand tightens, and I know he's about to crush it.

"No!" The word bursts from me, panicked. "Don't move! Don't do it!"

Instantly, his body relaxes. He looks at me, confused, waiting for an answer. But I don't give one.

The gecko lives.

Without another word, I grab my teacher's bag and rush out of the room. I need to get away—from that awful, unnatural thing, from the chaos slithering into my home. I need order. I need normalcy. I need the clear, steady rhythm of a school bell marking the beginning and end of things.

But my legs take me somewhere else.

Sometimes, your body knows where you need to go before your mind does. My feet carry me, not toward school, but down the familiar streets that lead to my mother's house. The April sun beats down, and I try to dodge the burning light, longing for the cool shade inside her home.

She'll be happy to see me, I tell myself. Isn't that what mothers do? Feel joy when their daughters visit, even if that daughter is me?

"What a surprise!" she says as she opens the door.

She's wearing one of Father's old bathrobes, her small frame lost in the oversized fabric. I pause in the doorway, taking her in. This woman who carried me, who gave me life. I remember the night in the cemetery, the way the earth groaned and trembled as I shaped Saul, as if it, too, was in labor. I remember how my own body shook from the weight of creation. Bringing something into the world always takes something from you—something you never get back.

"Is everything okay?" I ask, forcing a smile. I want this visit to be different, to keep it from turning into another strained conversation.

"Uh… I don't know," she says, hesitating. Then, more firmly, "You look wonderful, Telma."

Telma, five years old.

She sits on the floor, her little braids sticking out, her big eyes filled with questions only children are brave enough to ask.

"Mommy," she says in her small, hopeful voice, "is Nili pretty?"

Mother's hands fumble with the jars on her dressing table. She rubs a sharp-smelling cream into her neck, her eyes fixed on anything but her daughter.

"Yes," she says at last, her voice flat. "Nili is very pretty."

Telma waits. She already knows how the story should go. Every fairy tale, every bedtime tale, ends the same way: But you are even prettier, my lovely daughter.

She waits as her mother massages the cream into her skin. Waits, because she still believes the words will come.

But they don't.

"And… what about me?" she finally asks, the pause stretching too long.

"You are, too," Mother says, and just like that, the words carve themselves into her heart, becoming a secret definition of ugly.

Now, standing here in her home, I feel something different. A warmth, unfamiliar but bright, starts to grow inside me. It blends with the spark Saul has awakened in me. For the first time, I think maybe— just maybe—I might be beautiful.

I smile at Mother, a real smile. But the moment fades as I take in the room around us.

It's a mess.

Dirty glasses pile up on the table, old newspapers litter the floor. A once-thriving plant in the corner has shriveled, its brown leaves scattered. The floor is sticky in places, and a crumpled wrapper peeks out from beneath the carpet.

"What happened to your voice?" Mother asks suddenly, her forehead creased with concern. She picks up a glass, her movements slow and careful, like someone who is afraid to break.

"It'll be fine," I say, trying to sound reassuring. "But you don't look well. Are you sick?"

"I don't know," she murmurs, avoiding my eyes. "What about you?"

Me?

What could I possibly say?

That my heart is bursting with something wild and new? That I have found love—strange, messy, impossible to ignore? That my bed is stained with earth, proof of the life I have created?

But I look at her, wrapped in that old bathrobe, her body small, her voice uncertain, and I say nothing.

We sit together in the dusty living room, sipping tea in silence. Her hands are delicate, her spoon clinking softly against the cup. The frailty in her movements unsettles me. I have always known my mother was fragile in spirit, but now, for the first time, I see that her body is fragile, too.

"Your father wanted to take me to the hospital," Mother says after a long pause.

"Why didn't you go?"

She doesn't answer. But we both know why. She has always avoided doctors, trusting them only when she had no other choice. The only time she let Father take her was when she gave birth to me. "You came out in under a minute!" she always brags. I never understood why I was in such a hurry.

I try to remember a time when my mother was sick, but nothing comes to mind. It was always me—sniffling, running fevers, catching every little illness. But now, here she is, looking so small and frail. She has always been delicate in spirit, but her body was strong. Not anymore. Her pale face looks tired, worn down.

And then I smell it.

Not the usual scent of dust and clutter, but something else. Something sickly sweet, thick and heavy in the air. It fills my nose, making my stomach turn.

"Where does it hurt?" I ask, my voice catching.

"Down here," she says, folding her arms over her stomach. "The pain is strong, but I'll be fine." She gives me a faint smile, like she's trying to reassure me. But it only makes me more uneasy. The smell lingers, curling around me like something alive. My stomach churns. I swallow hard to keep from gagging.

"Look what Tzilla brought me yesterday," she says suddenly, pointing to a ceramic vase on the table. It's white and shiny, covered in red peach hearts. Their shape reminds me too much of raw, sliced meat. She beams with pride. "Isn't it beautiful?"

I barely glance at it. The overwhelming smell is pressing in on me, making it hard to focus.

"Mother," I say, forcing my voice to stay calm, "I think you're really sick. Very, very sick."

She waves a hand dismissively. "Oh, nonsense. You got better, didn't you? And look at you now. You're so pretty."

She laughs—a light, girlish sound. "Maybe when I get better, I'll look as good as you."

Two compliments in one hour. My whole life, I've waited for even one. And now, they spill from her so casually.

Warmth spreads through me, filling me with something strange and powerful. For the first time, I feel like I could do anything—set fire to the world and build it better than before. There is nothing Telma cannot do.

Mother watches me, studying my face, her hand resting absently on her stomach.

"Do you have a boyfriend, Telma dear?" she asks, her voice playful.

My eyes flick to the door of my old bedroom. It hasn't changed. The same faded floral bedsheet, the same thin mattress, untouched for years. Even now, it holds the quiet loneliness of my childhood.

"Why do you ask?" I say carefully.

"Because you seem different," she says, narrowing her eyes slightly. "And you're acting differently."

"Different how?" I ask, curiosity creeping in. It's always unsettling to hear how others see you—to realize the version of yourself in their minds might not match the one in yours. But I still want to know.

"I don't know," she says, her gaze drifting. "You just suddenly seem so concerned about me. And earlier, when my stomach hurt really bad and I kind of convulsed, I noticed something… You flinched. Like you felt it, too."

Her words hit harder than I expect, sending a sharp twist through my chest.

"I remember how I felt when I fell in love with your father," she says, her voice softening with nostalgia. A dreamy, almost foolish look crosses her face, and I have to fight the urge to roll my eyes.

"I just wanted to do nice things for everyone," she goes on. "I even helped old ladies cross the street, whether they wanted to or not." She laughs lightly, lost in the past. I wish she'd stop. Something about seeing love on her face feels… wrong.

"And now here you are," she says, her voice warm. "Being so nice to me today. I thought maybe you were in love, too."

Her face suddenly flushes, as if every tiny vein beneath her skin has burst at once. And just like that, my own cheeks burn in response. My throat tightens.

Is this what she considers kindness? A short visit, a lukewarm cup of tea, a few half-hearted questions about her health?

Why does she settle for so little?

She finishes the last drops of her tea and gives me a small, grateful smile. I can't bring myself to return it.

I look away, my hands twisting in my lap.

Yes, Mother. I am being nice to you.

Nice at your expense.

Chapter 26

Your bed feels enormous. You lie in the middle of it, small and alone, like a single pea lost in a sea of white sheets. Your mind drifts, empty, unable to focus on the one thought that has haunted you since you walked through the door. From the moment you scrubbed the soot from your skin to the second you collapsed into the pillows, the question has lingered, unspoken but heavy:

Will you ever see him again?

Could it be that he's hurt, burned, turned to ash like the little dolls swallowed by fire? The thought lands with a dull thud: today is Lag B'Omer, the holiday of flames. Maybe the fire has taken another sacrifice—another creation of yours, lost to the heat.

No. That can't be. He isn't gone. You are the only one who can destroy him, and you haven't. Not yet. Not now. Not now.

But the fear doesn't leave you. You want him here, beside you, his familiar warmth filling the empty space in your bed. You want him. And yet... what if he never comes back?

Never comes back.

The words settle in your mind like cold, hard stone. He's not coming back. Ever. How foolish you were to believe otherwise.

You start to doubt yourself. Did you really see him at school, or was it just a trick of your imagination, something your heart made up? If he was there, why didn't he come home with you? Where is he now?

Your thoughts race, running in circles. What is he doing out there, this creature of earth and fire? What is he seeing? What is he thinking? But you're not afraid for him. You know he can survive. Life with you, Telma, has surely prepared him for anything.

So why hasn't he come back?

Has he figured you out? Seen the worst parts of you—the selfishness, the neediness, the fears you try to hide? Maybe he finally understands just how much you rely on him, how dependent you are. The same insecure thoughts that haunt women when their men leave creep into your mind. You can almost hear him saying it: It's not you, it's me.

The irony doesn't escape you.

Your sleep is restless. You toss and turn in the empty bed, your body searching for the weight of someone beside you. How strange that you got used to his presence so fast. And now, as the hours drag on, the truth settles in: you will sleep alone again. Just as you always have. Just as you always will.

Then—

A sound.

You jolt awake.

What was that?

The house feels different, as if it's floating, untethered. Outside, the silver moon stares through the window. It always seems full when you are uneasy, its pale light cold and judging. You remember how it glowed at Grandma Gerta's funeral, watching as if it knew every secret. It was full the night you created Saul, too, a silent witness to everything.

And now? Now it hangs slightly deflated, like something unfinished. How you hate that glowing orb. Isn't there a story that says the moon was once part of the Earth before breaking away? Like all things that leave, it never really disappears. It just circles endlessly, watching.

Then—

A noise. Slow, heavy footsteps dragging across the floor.

Your heart leaps.

Could it be?

Is he back?

A thousand thoughts crash together, making you dizzy. What will you say? How will you welcome him?

Your body betrays you. You squeeze your eyes shut, pretending to sleep. Really, Telma? This is what you've stooped to? Childish games? Yet you can't move, can't bring yourself to make things easy for him. Somewhere deep inside, that insecure part of you demands that he prove himself.

Then—

Warmth.

Before you see him, you feel him. The heat of his body presses against the air, heavy and inescapable. He stands over you, silent. You shrink under the weight of his presence. He is watching you, studying you.

Does he still think you're beautiful? Did he ever?

Your mind spirals. Has he seen other women while he was gone? Soft lips, warm skin, curves that aren't yours? What if, now that he's back, he's comparing you to what he's seen?

The panic takes hold, and your eyes snap open.

He is there.

Towering over you, unmoving. His eyes locked on yours.

You force a small, hesitant smile.

Nothing.

He doesn't react. His face is still, unreadable.

You try again, widening your smile, stretching it so far it almost hurts. You bare your gums in desperation, hoping to break through his silence.

Still, nothing.

Something cold trickles through you. A flicker of doubt.

Why does he feel different? Have you done something wrong?

Then—

Without warning, he moves.

His hands reach for you, lifting you effortlessly into his arms. He carries you like you weigh nothing. His strength should be comforting, but instead—

The smell of smoke lingers on him.

It coils around you, seeping into your thoughts. You should feel relieved, but his touch is stiff, distant. He holds you like an object, not a person.

You don't cry, though maybe you should. His grip isn't gentle. He doesn't cradle you the way you imagined. He carries you with purpose, detached, as if you are nothing but dust in his hands.

The moonlight slices through the room like a blade, sharp and bright.

To your left, a tiny sound—

A laugh.

Your eyes dart to the source.

The needlepoint fawn.

Its stitched mouth twisted in a mocking grin.

You swallow hard, forcing yourself to breathe.

Imagine, you tell yourself.

Imagine you are a bride, carried by her husband. Imagine he holds you close because he wants to, because you are his and he is yours.

Ignore the doubt creeping in.

Isn't this what you always wanted?

Saul is yours now. Forever.

All you have to do is wait.

But Saul doesn't stop. He carries you up the narrow attic stairs, his steps steady, his movements stiff and unnatural. In the small, dusty space, he sets you down among old shelves and forgotten things, like a package dropped at its final destination.

Your bare feet land on broken glass—shattered jam jars. The sharp edges dig into your skin, and you feel warm blood mix with the sticky remains of peaches. The metallic scent of blood and the thick, sugary smell of fruit fill your nose. The room tilts, your tongue heavy in your mouth.

Then—

You jolt awake.

A sharp, jarring sound cuts through the silence. Your heart pounds. What is that? You strain to listen.

Fool.

It's the telephone.

You're still in bed, alone. Outside, the sky glows with the soft pinks and golds of dawn, the horizon brushed with the faded colors of an old painting.

And Saul—he isn't here.

You can't stay in bed another second. The sheets are cold. The floor is colder. The idea of answering the phone doesn't even cross your mind. Whoever it is, it can't be him.

You drift into Grandpa's office, your eyes landing on the old photographs.

There's your grandmother—her lips curved into a smile, her bright eyes filled with a joy that seems almost too much. Her frozen expression feels like a riddle, something hidden beneath the black-and-white surface.

What you wouldn't give to know when that picture was taken. Before or after she created the golem?

But does it matter?

The answer is already written all over your face, pressed into the empty bed you just left behind.

If Grandma Gerta were here, what would she say? You can almost hear the sharp, teasing words she'd throw at you, the knowing look in her eyes. You hate the scattered pieces of her that linger inside you, unfinished and unsatisfying. You want to erase that smug little smile from her picture—or maybe, just maybe, take it for yourself.

Because this is your story now, isn't it? Not hers.

Right?

But you never asked how her story ended, did you? You were too busy being a child, laughing at the edges of her tales, never realizing they held something more. And now, look at you. Alone. Wrapped in an old bathrobe, clutching faded photographs like some desperate fool.

And then—

A sound.

The slow, dragging weight of heavy footsteps.

You freeze.

The steps are steady, deliberate—undeniably his. They stop outside your door.

The air shifts.

The door bursts open. A rush of heat follows.

Saul.

For a moment, the world tilts. Your head swims. Is this real?

But yes—he is here. His presence pulls everything into focus, anchoring you. Those dark, knowing eyes have seen so much. And yet, they still found their way back to you.

You don't ask why. You don't question anything. You don't even notice the photographs slipping from your trembling hands.

You just run to him.

A wild, reckless joy surges through you, raw and overwhelming. It is the kind of joy that always comes before a great fall—but you don't care. His arms close around you, strong and sure. He holds you tightly, and in that embrace, there is only one truth: he came back.

This—this moment—is the greatest gift he has ever given you. Second only to the kiss you still dream of but have yet to receive.

Your face tilts upward. The space between you disappears. His breath is warm against your lips. You don't hesitate. You want him to take everything—every breath, every piece of you—into himself.

His hand moves, fingers brushing against your lips, tasting of earth, of life and death entwined. You close your eyes, surrendering.

The scent of smoke lingers between you. Heat flares against your skin, flames licking at the edges of the moment. Your hair stirs as if caught in an unseen wind, your body dusted with soot.

Your lips part, waiting—

Then—

The door slams open.

The force rattles the walls, sending flecks of plaster crumbling to the floor.

Simon stands in the doorway, his expression cold, his presence thick with something awful.

"I just came from the hospital," he says, voice flat.

A pause. A breath.

"Your mother is dead."

Two.

Your mind splits cleanly into two.

One part absorbs the words with a strange, empty calm.

Your mother is dead.

The finality of it is absolute.

Dead.

Mother.

Dead.

But what does that even mean? The weight of it doesn't fully sink in, clouded by your own confusion.

Yet, part of you is completely aware of what's happening right in front of you.

Simon and Saul are staring at each other for the first time.

Their eyes lock above your head, the air between them crackling with tension. The room feels like a storm about to break.

Simon's fingers twitch at his side.

Your mother is dead.

Saul doesn't flinch.

Dead.

His lips press into a firm line, his eyes narrowing in silent focus. Poor Mother—even in death, she cannot hold your full attention.

The standoff continues. A battle with no words, just two men locked in an invisible struggle. You stand in the middle, dazed, your mind unable to keep up with what's unfolding.

Then—

Simon moves.

In a sudden, shocking motion, he thrusts his hand into Saul's mouth.

His mouth.

The same mouth that was supposed to kiss you. The one you had dreamed about, waited for. The mouth that holds the slip of paper— the one thing keeping Saul alive.

A violent shudder runs through you. This is wrong. This is violence in its purest form.

"I told you," Simon snarls, his face red with anger. "If you can't do it, I will!"

His hand pushes deeper, his fingers grasping wildly.

Then—

A scream.

Raw. Animalistic. Terrifying.

Your hands fly to your own mouth, but the scream isn't yours.

It's Simon's.

Blood drips from his arm, thick and dark, pooling onto the floor.

Saul has bitten him.

You've never seen Saul's teeth before. Never knew how sharp they could be. But now, his mouth is open, and his teeth gleam in the dim light like the edge of a blade.

Still, Simon doesn't back down. Even through the pain, he lunges again, his uninjured hand reaching forward. "I'll kill you!" he shouts, voice wild with rage.

Saul doesn't hesitate. His hands clamp around Simon's throat, powerful and unyielding. He starts to squeeze.

But he doesn't take his eyes off you.

Even as Simon struggles, gasping for air, clawing at Saul's arms—Saul is watching you.

His hands tighten. Simon's face turns red, then purple. His breaths come in weak, choked gasps. Yet even in his final moments, he doesn't stop fighting. He grips Saul's lower lip and pulls, his fingers digging deep.

Somewhere, a clock chimes softly, out of place in the chaos.

You watch, frozen.

This feels familiar. Like something you've already imagined before. Like a memory, playing out in real time.

Two men, fighting to the death.

But neither one is looking at each other.

They are only looking at you.

Simon gurgles, his voice barely there. "Tell him… tell him to stop. He's killing me…"

The words hit like a strike to your chest.

You hesitate.

If you tell Saul to stop, Simon will live—and win.

You can already picture it. Simon's hand tearing the slip of paper from Saul's mouth. Saul's body breaking apart, crumbling into nothing but dirt and dust.

Gone.

You don't want that.

Simon's eyes roll back. His hands go limp. His tongue slips from his mouth, his skin going ghostly pale.

A spike of panic shoots through you.

Before you can stop yourself, the words spill out:

"Enough, Saul! Stop! Leave him be!"

The moment you say it, you know it's a mistake.

Saul flinches.

His whole body stiffens, his grip faltering just slightly. His eyes snap to yours, full of something unreadable. Hurt? Betrayal? Sadness?

You can't tell.

But Simon sees his chance.

With a desperate burst of energy, he lunges again. His hand shoots toward Saul's mouth—

Saul moves faster.

His hands tighten. His arms shift.

Then—

A sickening crack.

Simon's arm bends the wrong way. Bone snaps through skin, white against red.

Simon falls to the floor, screaming in agony. His body twists in pain, his broken arm hanging uselessly at his side. The air fills with the sound of his raw, jagged cries.

You shut your eyes, blocking it out.

When you open them, nothing has changed.

The two men remain where they are.

Saul, standing tall, silent, his expression unreadable.

Simon, crumpled on the floor, writhing in pain.

Their eyes are still locked, a battle that hasn't ended.

You can't take it anymore.

The weight of it all is crushing you, pulling at you from both sides, demanding something from you that you no longer have to give.

You turn and run. Let them destroy each other, let their anger consume them both. You don't care anymore. You just need to get away.

Your mother is dead.

The night air is hot and dry, stinging your tired eyes. You walk quickly, putting as much distance as possible between yourself and the suffocating weight of home. But as you move through the familiar streets—past the rustling orange trees, past the laughing children—you realize something.

The fight between Saul and Simon isn't just happening back in your apartment. It's inside you, too. It has always been there. And it will never truly end.

At the end of the street, a figure steps out from the shadows. The moonlight catches her hair, making it glow like a halo.

Nili.

"I heard about your mother," she says when you reach her. Her voice is quiet, almost gentle. "I'm so sorry."

You study her, surprised by the sudden connection you feel. For the first time, she doesn't seem like a rival, someone untouchable and distant. She is just Nili—human, flawed, as breakable as you.

Something unspoken passes between you. You both come from the same tangled roots, tied to the same complicated history. The same blood, the same strange pull that neither of you can explain.

"How did you find out?" Your voice sounds flat, distant.

"Simon told me," she says.

His name stirs nothing in you. No anger, no sadness. Just exhaustion.

"We were supposed to go to your place together," she adds.

But you barely hear her. Your mind is back in that apartment, trapped with the two men you left behind, locked in their endless fight.

"He's already there."

"Can I go now?" Your voice is hoarse, thin.

"No. Not yet."

She reaches for you suddenly, her fingers closing tightly around your elbow. Her grip is firm, almost desperate.

"Telma," she says, her voice shaking now. She squeezes your arm like she's afraid you'll disappear if she lets go. Her wide eyes hold something you don't expect—fear. Real, raw fear.

You don't ask what's wrong. You already know.

"Everything will be fine," you whisper, though you don't believe it. The words feel empty, lifeless. Your body feels unbearably heavy, your mind foggy with exhaustion. You want to collapse right here on the pavement, let the heat of the ground seep into you while Nili stands over you, guarding the world from pressing in.

"I'm going to my father's house," you say suddenly, the words surprising even you. You haven't thought about him once tonight. The guilt is sharp and sudden.

"I can come with you," Nili offers, uncertain. You can tell she doesn't want to be alone either.

"All right." Your voice is barely a whisper.

You walk together, two shadows stretching long behind you in the dim light. The wind tugs at the ribbons in your hair, playful, reminding you of something long past—two little girls, stepping carefully in their best white shoes, side by side, following a path they cannot change.

Your hearts beat in time, echoing a sorrowful, familiar rhythm:

Two gray eyes, two lips, a heart, a hollow place

Which is prettier? It doesn't matter anymore.

Your father's house is filled with darkness.

The air is thick, pressing down on you, smothering. You lift your eyes to the ceiling as if looking for an escape, but the windows are shut tight. Even the moon is locked out, its cold light denied entry. Maybe it isn't worthy of witnessing what's inside.

Maybe you aren't worthy either.

You don't want the moon's judgment, not tonight. You don't want it to see you lying beside Saul in silence. A silence so deep, so heavy, that it's worse than anger, worse than resentment. This silence is something else entirely. A void.

Saul's breath is steady beside you, deep and slow.

Your mother's breath has ended.

Her last moments, her final exhale, are part of the air now. They linger in this room, slipping into Saul's lungs, into yours, mixing, fading.

You wonder how many of her breaths touched his. How many still linger here, unseen, waiting.

Who will be next?

You see flashes of your father in your mind—his lost, broken expression as he wandered aimlessly through the house, hollow and empty. His wide, vacant eyes, his voice barely a whisper, saying her name just once before falling silent. Another person in your life whose lips have sealed shut, as if words no longer matter.

Deep inside, you know with absolute certainty that Saul is not evil. This isn't a guess—it's something you know. He could have hurt you countless times, could have destroyed the people around you, could have crushed Simon completely if he wanted to. But he didn't. He held back. Doesn't that mean something?

Then why, Telma, do you still feel this fear twisting inside you? Why does his presence feel like it carries something dark and dangerous?

Could it be that the real problem isn't Saul?

Could it be you?

Your own selfishness, your greed, your unwillingness to let go? Maybe it's time to stop looking outward for the cause and face the truth about yourself.

But you can't. You won't. You don't even want to try.

You lie beside Saul, the silence so heavy it feels like it's pressing down on your chest. Your whole life has been about avoiding things—avoiding choices, avoiding responsibility. You've always searched for the path of least resistance, the option that required no real decision.

But now, the moment of choice is coming. You can feel it closing in, suffocating.

Soon, you'll have to decide.

You'll have to face the truth about what you really want.

And yet—

You can't give him up.

No. No, no. The word pounds in your head, louder each time.

But how much longer can you defend him? How much longer can you stand by him while the people around you suffer? What if you are next?

Even if you wanted to end this, how could you? Saul has grown beyond you, become stronger than anything you could ever hope to control.

And yet...

You turn toward him in the darkness, searching his face for answers. Hoping for some kind of sign, a hint about what to do next. But he gives you nothing.

Just silence.

The doubt creeps in, slow and steady, like a shadow at the edge of your mind. How did he get so strong? And yet, why does he always come back? Was that his choice? Or was it because of you—because of the slip of paper hidden under his tongue, the words you placed there that night in the cemetery?

Did he return because he wanted to... or because you forced him to?

You shift closer, hesitating before leaning over him. His breath is warm against your skin, thick with the scent of damp earth and something faintly human. A shiver runs through you, a mix of familiarity and unease.

Slowly, you reach out, your fingers trembling as they brush against his face.

You trace the curve of his brow, smooth and unmarked. Your fingertips drift lower, brushing over his closed eyelids—so peaceful, so perfect, as if carved by a sculptor's hand. Then his nose, the shallow dip just below it, and finally—

His lips.

Warm. Familiar. But also foreign, unreadable.

Your fingers linger there, tracing their shape, feeling the strange contrast between softness and strength. His breathing deepens beneath your touch, but his body stays completely still. He doesn't move. He doesn't react.

And yet, your own breath hitches, uneven.

Why does this moment stir something inside you, Telma?

Could it be that you like this?

You let your fingertips glide over the smooth heat of his lips, marveling at the sensation—silk and fire. A flicker of boldness ignites inside you, and before you can stop yourself, the tip of your finger slips between them.

Slowly.

Carefully.

Inside, his lips are soft but strangely dry, lacking the warmth of a human mouth. The feeling is alien, unfamiliar. A strange thrill shoots through you, tangled with an unbearable tension. You are so close now, close to the very thing that makes him him.

But then—

Your fingertip meets resistance.

His teeth.

Sharp. Unmoving. A barrier, locked tight.

You hesitate.

Just a little farther…

You push gently, testing, pressing past—

A violent explosion of movement.

A force slams into you, hurling you backward like a rag doll.

You crash into the closet door with a sickening thud, your body crumbling to the floor.

Stars burst behind your eyes—green, purple, dazzling, blinding. Your head spins, the room tilting and twisting around you.

Pain crashes over you like a wave, sharp and merciless.

Your mouth fills with blood, hot and metallic, pooling on your tongue. Your nose feels like it's on fire, throbbing with a deep, unbearable ache. The entire left side of your face burns, pain radiating in waves.

It hurts.

It hurts so much.

And suddenly—

A memory surges forward.

You are ten years old again, small hands reaching for the cookie jar on the highest shelf.

The sweet smell of cookies fills the air, and you stretch higher, fingers just barely grazing the lid.

Then—

You slip.

You fall.

The jar crashes down with you, heavy glass colliding with your face.

The pain is instant.

The sharp, shattering crack of your nose breaking.

The sting of tears.

The sound of cookies scattering around you, a cruel, mocking rain.

And now, lying here, bleeding, hurting, you realize—

This is how it always is, Telma.

Everything you reach for.

Everything you want.

It always finds a way to break you.

Chapter 30

Saul's lips press against mine, and suddenly, it's as if my entire body opens up at once. A flood of warmth, damp earth, and something deeper rushes over me. I hear voices in the distance, but their words blur into nothing. The world around me disappears, swallowed by this kiss—his kiss.

It takes over everything. I feel like I no longer exist as a person, only as a mouth. My tongue moves, brushing against my teeth, but I don't feel Saul's. Inside him, everything is soft, wet, endless. It's as if my tongue has slipped deep inside him, into a space I don't understand.

Where does all this moisture come from? What part of him holds so much of it?

The sound of collapsing buildings echoes in the distance. I taste something sweet—peaches, maybe. But I know it isn't real. None of it is. This moment, this kiss, is all that matters. This is what I have been waiting for. This is what a kiss should be.

And now, I have it.

I don't feel like myself anymore—I am part of him. I melt into him, into this kiss, into the gift he is giving me. He knows exactly what I need, always has. He must have realized that I could never bring myself to take the slip of paper from his mouth, never do what needed to be done.

So now, Saul is doing it for me.

I press closer, my heart pounding. Would I ever have been able to make this sacrifice on my own?

Saul, Saul, Saul. I love him.

Words swirl around us, unspoken but alive, fluttering like butterflies. Our lips stay locked, carrying a silent conversation no one else will ever understand. My whole body aches, tight with something I can't name, but suddenly, I see Saul more clearly than ever before.

Now, I understand.

I understand why I reached into the earth that night, why I created him, why he exists. And why I do, too.

Love.

Then—I feel it.

At the very edge of my tongue.

The slip of paper.

It lies there, soaked, hidden beneath Saul's tongue. My tongue brushes against it, and a shock runs through me. The texture is strange—elastic, alive. It tastes sharp, like metal, like blood. I can't move it. Every time I touch it, another jolt shoots through me, making me tremble.

I try to pull away, but Saul doesn't let me go. He holds me against him, his lips pressing harder, firmer.

And then—

Does he smile?

Is there the slightest curve to his lips?

Time stretches. I don't know if I am pulling the slip of paper toward me or if Saul is pushing it forward, but slowly—achingly slowly—it moves.

It slides between us, slipping past our lips, brushing against our teeth. It crosses from him to me, gliding into my mouth.

It settles beneath my tongue.

A perfect fit.

Thank You for Reading

Dear Reader,

We hope this timeless classic has sparked your imagination and enriched your literary journey. Now that you've turned the final page, we want to share a vision for the future of reading—one where every classic you've ever wanted to explore is at your fingertips, in a format that best suits your life.

We'd like to invite you to gain immediate, unlimited digital & audiobook access to hundreds of the most treasured literary classics ever written—along with the option to secure deluxe paperback, hardcover & box set editions at printing cost. Together, we can spark a new global literary renaissance alongside our small, independent publishing house called "The Library of Alexandria."

Thousands of years ago, the Library of Alexandria stood as a beacon of knowledge—until it was lost to history. We aim to reignite that spirit of preservation and discovery right now, in the modern age—only this time, it's accessible to all, in every language and every format.

Picture a world where every timeless classic, novel, poem, or philosophical treatise is not only available to read but also updated for today's readers—modernized, translated into any language or dialect, and ready to enjoy in any format you choose, whether that is in an eBook, audiobook, paperback, or deluxe hardcover & box set version a printing cost.

By joining our movement to rebuild the modern Library of Alexandria, you become part of an unprecedented mission to offer:

- **Unlimited Audiobook & eBook Access to the Greatest Classics of All Time**

  Instantly explore thousands of legendary works, from Plato and Shakespeare to Jane Austen and Leo Tolstoy. All are instantly ready to read or listen to, giving you a complete literary universe at your fingertips.

- **Paperback & Deluxe Editions at Printing Costs:**

  Purchase any title in a paperback, deluxe hardbound, or deluxe boxset edition at printing costs, shipped right to your doorstep. Curate your personal library of Alexandria with editions worthy of display—crafted to last, designed to captivate, and delivered straight to your door.

- **Modern translations for Contemporary Readers in all languages and dialects**

  Discover a vast selection of classics reimagined in clear, current language—no more struggling with outdated phrases or obscure references. Next to the original versions, we aim to offer translations in as many languages and dialects as possible.

  As we continue our translation efforts and add new languages, readers everywhere can connect with these works as if they were written today. By bridging linguistic divides, you're contributing to ensuring that these timeless stories become more meaningful, accessible, and inspiring for people across the globe.

- **Your Personal Library of Alexandria:**

  Over the months and years, you'll curate a unique physical archive of classics—each volume a testament to your taste, curiosity, and love of knowledge. It's not just about owning books—it's about curating a cultural legacy you'll cherish and pass down for generations to come.

- **Join a Global Literary Renaissance:**

  Your support fuels an ongoing mission: allowing us to reinvest in offering deluxe print editions (including special boxsets) at their true cost, broaden the range of available formats and translations, and extend the reach of these works to new audiences worldwide. By joining today, you're not just preserving a legacy of masterpieces; you set in motion a powerful wave of literary accessibility.

  We are more than a publisher—we're a movement, and we can't do it alone. Your support lets us scale our mission, preserving and reimagining history's greatest works for tomorrow's readers.

Become a Torchbearer of knowledge.

Thank you for picking up this book and allowing us into your literary journey. As you turn the pages, know that you're part of something larger: a global effort to keep these stories alive, share their wisdom across borders and generations, and spark a true cultural revival for the modern era.

If this resonates with you—please consider taking the next step by visiting:

www.libraryofalexandria.com

With gratitude and a shared love of knowledge,

The Modern Library of Alexandria Team

Visit:

www.libraryofalexandria.com

Or scan the code below: